# Executive Protection

# Executive Protection

**Dr. S. Subramanian**

*Former*

Director General : C.R.P.F. & N.S.G.
Joint Director : Intelligence Bureau
DIG : Central Bureau of Investigation (CBI)
Director : National Police Academy
Minister : Embassy of India, Germany

**1998**

**MANAS PUBLICATIONS**

NEW DELHI-110 002

**MANAS PUBLICATIONS**
(Publishers, Distributors & Exporters)
4819/XI, Varun House, Mathur Lane,
24, Ansari Road, Darya Ganj,
New Delhi-110002 (INDIA)
Ph.: 3260783, 3265523, 2523865
Fax : 011 - 3272766 & 2927854
E-Mail : manas.vkgarg@axcess.net.in



**ISBN** 81-7049-079-0



*First Published 1998*

*Typeset at*
Innovative Processors
New Delhi-110 002

*Printed in India at*
Print Perfect, Delhi
and Published by Mrs. Suman Lata for
Manas Publications, 4819/XI, Varun House,
Mathur Lane, 24, Ansari Road, Darya Ganj,
New Delhi-110002 (INDIA)

This Book is Dedicated to the Personnel of:

* The Special Protection Group
* Special Ranger Groups of the National Security Guards
* VIP Security Detachments of Intelligence Departments of the States and Union Territories in India
* Who by their devotion to Duty, Sacrifice and Hard work Protect the Dignitories entrusted to their corps.

# Preface

Business executives and industrialists are increasingly becoming the target of attack by diverse criminal elements like Terrorists, Extremists, Organised Crime, Petty Criminals and others. Main reason for this attack being the perception, that the Executives or their Organisations have the capacity to pay large sums of money as ransom or they are capable of influencing favourable political decisions. Most of the executives are blissfully unaware of this ever present danger and do not take any steps to protect themselves.

This Book aims to create an awareness among the executives and to provide them with :

(*a*) Basic knowledge about how the miscreants operate and to highlight the point that these attacks are not arbitrary nor the result of angry reaction to events, but a well planned, directed and calculated operations;

(*b*) To provide the executives with skills to create personal protection arrangements at their homes, offices and while they are on the move;

(*c*) To inculcate the habit of taking defensive actions as a matter of routine in every day life thereby denying the opportunity to the miscreants to cause harm; and

(*d*) To reinforce an attitude of self confidence and capacity to face adversities.

Case histories have been provided to highlight and reinforce the above points.

Since Political Executives and Diplomats also face threats from the miscreants, though for political and reasons other than monetary, separate chapters to deal with this problem and protection arrangements for these dignitaries have been included.

This Book is the result of exhaustive study of the subject for over three decades and intense interaction with security professionals all over the world, who are the experts in the field personal protection. As an acknowledged authority on Personal Protection in India and the Founder Director of the Special Protection Group, which guards the Prime Minister of India, the author has drawn heavily on his personal experience.

A Book of this nature cannot be written without the advice and suggestions from many friends and security professionals. Constraints of space prevents me from recording individual vote of thanks.

I owe a special debt of thanks to:

* My wife, Smt.S.Jayalakshmi for her patience, understanding and encouragement;
* Shri G.Raj Reddy for secretarial and computer assistance, at all stages of the preparation of this Book; and
* Shri V.K.Garg, Director, Manas Publications for enthusing me to write this book and bringing out the same in a record time in an elegant and attractive format.

If this book helps the busy business executives to take precautions to protect themselves and their families, my labours would have been amply rewarded.

Dr.S.Subramanian

# Contents

*Preface* *vii*

## Part I

### Executive Protection

1. The Need **3**
2. Planning for Personal Protection **11**
3. Protective Arrangements at Home **17**
4. Security of Office and Workplace **27**
5. Meeting Threats During Road Journeys **35**
6. Protection During Air and Foreign Travel **47**
7. Managing a Crisis **54**
8. Hostage Negotiations **60**
9. Know Your Enemy **66**
10. Means of Destruction of the Miscreants **70**
11. Dealing with Threats from Explosives **75**
12. Case Studies of Kidnapping of Executives **82**
13. Protection for the Family **95**
14. Personal Protection Personnel - Bodyguard **99**

# Part II
## Diplomatic Protection

15. Protection of Diplomats 109
16. Case Studies 112

# Part III
## Protection of Political Executives

17. Sources of Threats 117
18. Principles of Protection 120
19. Arrangements for Specific Situations 126
20. Case Studies of Assasinations and Attempts 128

# Part IV
## Miscellaneous Threats to Business

21. Threats from Special Interest Groups 165
22. Threats to contaminate Consumer Products 167

*Select Bibliography* *171*

*Index* *173*

# PART I

## Executive Protection

# 1 The Need

BUSINESS EXECUTIVES and industrialists are increasingly becoming the target of attack of Terrorists, Radicals, Organised Crime, Dismissed Employees, Disturbed Individuals, Environmental Activists and small time criminals, due to popular perception that they or their Corporations have the capacity to pay large sums of money or capable of influencing political decisions. Kidnapping for Ransom has become a multi-billion dollar industry. Unless the executives are aware of the threats and take suitable preventive steps, sooner or later, they are bound to become victims. In this book, we are using the term miscreants to describe all these diverse criminal elements. We shall outline the processes that generate this crime and suggest remedial actions to be taken.

## Sources of Threat and Definitions

### Abduction

Abduction is defined as forcible and illegal carrying off a person for any purpose.

This is an ancient form of crime as old as civilisation. In the early days, it was resorted to for amorous purposes or to force the victim to accept personal or political decisions which are unpalatable. Often, the victim was manhandled and abused physically and mentally in the process.

## Short Term Abduction

This is a growing form of crime in the West. An executive, usually the one, who has access to cash resources, like a Bank Manager, is taken away at gun point and made to open the Safe and handover the money to the miscreants. As long as the victim cooperates, no harm will come to him. The captivity lasts usually for few hours and in very rare cases over 24 hours.

## Kidnapping

Kidnapping is defined as the abduction of victim or victims to an unknown destination, to be held there for as long as may be necessary, to extort concessions— financial, political and sometimes for publicity value. The term is derived from 'Kid-nabbing' abduction of the child, a very common form of crime for money in the 19th century.

This is the worst form of crime. The victim is under the sentence of death for an indefinite period. It has devastating ill effects on the victim.

## Anti-Development Abductions

Abduction of foreign personnel and technicians, usually in remote places by miscreants to extract concessions from their Governments on developmental and environmental issues.

## Hostage Taking

In this, the victims are held in a known location and under threat of personal violence, to extort political or other concessions. This is done mostly to gain publicity to the cause of miscreants. Normally, no ransom or money is demanded, though there have been some exceptions. The hostage takers are as much interested in the smooth termination of the affair as the hostages since their basic aim is publicity.

### Hijackings

Hijacking of Aircraft, Ships, Trains etc. is another form of hostage taking, to extract political concessions.

### Product Extortion

This is the malicious contamination of a popular product to create the fear of death or ill health in the minds of consumers. This is done to harass, damage, intimidate or coerce the manufacturers or distributors to pay large sums of money. It could take either the actual form of contamination or threat to contaminate the product. Usually, the miscreants tamper with few pieces of merchandise in widely dispersed geographical locations all over the country and threaten the victim firm, that if the money demanded is not paid, contaminated products will reach the consumers.

### Bomb Threats

An explosive device is placed in a manufacturing facility or a public place and the concerned are warned, that if money or concessions demanded are not paid or accepted, the location of the bomb will not be revealed and it will explode at the predetermined time.

### Personal Attack or Intimidation

Personal attack or intimidation of the Executive or members of his family are resorted to frighten the executive to leave the location. This is generally resorted to in respect of multi-nationals and foreign firms. Often, one can discern the hands of local business rivals in these episodes.

### Protection Rackets

The dominant miscreant group in the area, extracts money with threats of resorting to violence, vandalism and sabotage, if money is not paid. It is a well known fact, that in India, in the industrial areas, large amounts are paid by industries to local Mafia/organised crime as Protection Money.

Of all the above, the most persistent and ever present

threat to the executive is from Kidnapping, which will be discussed in greater detail below.

**Seven Phases of a Kidnapping**

A kidnapping can be carried out by a single miscreant or a well organised gang. In all cases, there are seven identifiable phases in the execution of the crime.

**Target Selection**

Kidnappings are well planned operations. As a first step, the miscreants undertake an elaborate research study of their potential targets. At this stage, the wealth of the individual or of his organisation become the prime consideration. Detailed data are collected about the targets and their economic worth is assessed. Then, the target's accessibility and the predictability of his movements are studied. Subsidiary factors like family history, wealthy connections and other details are obtained. Most of this information is available in published material like Society Chronicles, WHO is WHO, Magazines etc. Where necessary, public records are also consulted. Two or three targets, which are likely to give the maximum returns, are short listed.

**Reconnaissance and Surveillance**

Once the potential targets have been selected, in order to collect precise data about them, reconnaissance and surveillance are undertaken. Surveillance would include placing static observers near the residence, office and places of regular engagement and with the help of vehicles following the target on his movements. The aim is to collect meticulously voluminous data about the routines and habits of the targets. Detailed documentation about when the targets leave for office, what type of the car is driven either by the chauffeur or the target himself, where the target goes for lunch, what type of hobbies and external activities are undertaken by the target, etc. is done to determine a pattern in the activities.

Reconnaissance includes detailed physical survey of the

spots considered most suitable for the kidnapping, shortest route to the detention centre, escape routes, possible law enforcement response and how to counter them, and other relevant operational requirements. Many dummy runs and dress rehearsals are held to perfect the timings. A detailed Risk Analysis is undertaken to counter the consequences of unexpected complications and failure of the attempt.

The data thus collected, enables the kidnappers to finally select one target, as the most suitable from operational point of view.

## Abduction

Based on the results of the surveillance and reconnaissance, the day, time, place and method are decided for abduction. The determining factor will be the probability of success and getaway. Teams are constituted for various aspects of the operation like creating diversionary tactics, blocking the roads, plans to face any opposition from the victim as well as the onlookers, etc. and detailed plans are worked out for each task. The 'Hit Team' is trained in the handling of vehicles, suitable weapons are selected, drugs to make the victim unconscious, blind folds, handcuffs etc. are procured and assembled.

The actual abduction takes only a few seconds as the exercise has been meticulously planned and rehearsed several times. In a Research Study, it was found, that more than half of reported kidnappings took place when the target was commuting between residence and office; one fourth from the residence and less than ten per cent from the office/workplace. A substantial number took place when the target was returning from Parties and Social Functions late in the night. As an element of surprise is maintained, there is normally no resistance from the victim. Kidnappers do not use violence, except to make the victim obey their commands. They do not shoot and kill the victim, as a dead kidnap victim has no money value. Though, there could be some rough treatment at the time of actual abduction, once the victim has been secured, there will be no further violence. To avoid the possibility of a chase, the vehicles are often changed and the victim is taken to the predetermined hide-out.

**Detention in a Hide-Out**

When the kidnappings take place in urban areas, it is common for the kidnappers to hide the victim in the city itself for a few days and later shift him to a rural area. The victim will be blindfolded and taken in a circuitous route to the detention centre. The place of detention varies. There have been cases where the victims have been kept in sewers, caves, underground tunnels, abandoned mines, etc. The hostage is kept confined with least possibility of movement. He will be kept blindfolded and often ear phones are thrust into the ears with continuous playing of music, to prevent the victim from overhearing conversations. Minimum amount of food will be supplied and toilet facilities may be non-existent or primitive. These unhygienic and severe hardships are often intentionally created to break the resolve of the victim.

Guards will be detailed to ensure that the victim does not escape. Normally, no violence will be used against the victim, unless he tries to escape or uses abusive language against the guards. Since the guards and the victim share the same primitive living conditions. When the detention gets prolonged, often the victim and the guard(s) become friendly and the victim begins to share the beliefs and the goals of the kidnappers. This is known as the 'Stockholm Syndrome'

Mutilation is seldom resorted to. Professional criminal gangs, sometimes cut off a finger or an ear and send them to the victim's family or friends, in order to convey the message of ruthlessness and to indicate the consequences that would follow if their dictates are not listened to. The Kidnappers know very well that any serious mutilation would need expert medical attention which cannot be provided due to risk of exposure. They are also aware that damaged goods will get minimum sale value in the business of kidnapping.

**Negotiations**

Over 90% of the recorded kidnappings were for cash ransom. At the first opportunity, the kidnappers will ask for an astronomical and impossible figure, will use very aggressive tones and postures. They also use psychological pressures like long silence without any communication and playing upon the medical needs of the victim, etc. Many means are used to contact the victim's family or firm. The kidnappers know that someone will negotiate a release deal and they also know precisely how much money can be extracted from the victim's family, Firm and Friends. Details of processes and stages of Negotiations are given in Chapter VIII.

**Ransom Collection**

Once the ransom has been agreed upon, details of the shape of the ransom, how it should be delivered, where, when and by whom are further discussed. This is a very crucial stage for the kidnappers. Any slip up will result in the whole operation becoming unproductive. Kidnappers go to elaborate lengths to ensure that they are not trapped by the police. They generally ask for the money to be paid in used currency notes of small denominations and ask the same to be dropped at a predetermined location. They take their own time and methods to pick up the money. Sometimes, in the West, money is asked to be deposited in numbered Swiss Bank Account. The ransom amount is immediately disbursed to the operational team members, rank and file and they are instructed to convert the same into normal market currency to prevent detection. Large amounts thus disappear in no time. Even when Kidnappers were located after painstaking investigation, it has not been possible to recover large chunks of the ransom.

**Release of Hostage**

More than 90% of the hostages have been released soon after the payment of ransom. Some delays occur due to the fact that the hostage has been secreted in a distant place. In few cases, deaths of victims have occurred after the payment of the ransom but these were due to extraneous factors and circumstances beyond the control of the kidnappers. As a general rule, kidnappers keep up their word. They perhaps want to build up a good business reputation.

A study of recorded kidnappings has revealed that 90% of the hostages survived the ordeal. Of those who died, many were killed in rescue attempts, in a few cases they died of natural causes and on occasions kidnappers killed them, when surrounded by police. There have been few cases where petty criminals organising the Kidnap, after collecting the ransom, killing the victim so that, he may not identify them to the police.

# 2

# Planning for Personal Protection

IT SHOULD BE NOTED that in the life of modern business executive, the risk of kidnapping is ever present. Like dealing with the ever present risk from fire to his industry or business, he should take positive steps to meet this risk. He should plan for his personal security and be mentally prepared to meet the worst situation. Specific steps to deal with the security arrangements at the residence, office, or while travelling etc. will be dealt with in detail in the subsequent chapters. Here, we deal with certain general principles applicable to all situations.

## Assessment of Threat

The executive should carefully consider all factors prevalent in his geographical area like, political situation, increasing domination of the society by the miscreants, effectiveness or otherwise of the Police to check organised crime and other miscreants, violent and destructive incidents in the industry and business environment and others. He should constantly update the data on these and determine whether the risk to his person is increasing or diminishing. He should take the help of security professionals and senior police officers in this assessment.

## Denial of Information to the Miscreants

We have noted that the basis of the miscreants selection of the target is the collection of information about the target. Therefore, a conscious effort should be made to deny this information. Care should be taken to scrutinise what goes into the In-House Journals, Press releases and so on. Secretaries and Public Relations staff are to be told not to give personal details and movement particulars of senior executives to unknown people. Family members and domestic help are to be briefed not to give these informations to unknown persons, particularly on the phone.

## Low Profile

The Executive should make a conscious effort to adopt a low profile and not to advertise his wealth. In public places like Hotels, Clubs and Bars, care should be taken not to discuss details of personal wealth and assets and no efforts should be made to boast about them. It should be remembered that the miscreants have their informants in these places, who are waiting to pickup such information. For the same reason, expensive cars and fittings attract attention.

## Observation

The Executive should learn to detect 'Surveillance'. There are basically three types of surveillance- Foot, Vehicle and Fixed.

Foot Surveillance usually consists of two individuals. They follow the target at a distance. Though they may change their clothes, the persons will be the same. If the executive is observant and notices the physical features of the strangers and newcomers moving in his vicinity, he will be able to locate the surveillance team. The Executive should concentrate on the physical characteristic of the surveillant. He should look back occasionally, to note whether they are being met by anyone else while on the job. When in a Restaurant or a public place, he should try to take a seat which does not provide a good view from outside and avoid sitting next to the glass windows or in the centre of the restaurant. He should not double back or look over the shoulder too often nor jump off the elevators or public transport and run into buildings with which he is not familiar. If there is an apprehension that harm may come to him, he should approach the nearest policeman or police station and with their help get a taxi to go home.

Vehicle Surveillance: Common place vehicles will be used. The surveillance can be detected by the persistent way the vehicle follows the vehicle of the executive. More than one vehicle will be deployed and there may be more than one passenger in them. Only indication that the vehicle is engaged in surveillance will be, that during nights, the interior light will not light up, when the doors are opened. As soon as the Executive parks his vehicle, the tail will also stop and one of the passengers will follow the executive on foot. To detect surveillance, a look out for suspicious vehicles going in front and following at the same pace, should be kept a note of. Particulars of such vehicles and passengers should be carefully noted. Evasive driving techniques should not be tried unless one has had specialised training in that art. Speed will result in one getting into unfamiliar localities and being trapped. Instead, one should drive straight into a Public place like a Police Station, Fire Station, Military installation etc. where lot of people with authority will be available.

Fixed Surveillance: This is done near the home or office by the surveillants assuming ordinary disguises like ice cream vendors, telephone and electric repairmen etc. Fixed surveillance posts are used for taking photographs. If possible, photographs of the surveillants should be taken from a distance. Physical description of the surveillants should be noted. No one should approach the surveillants nor stare at them nor show signs of recognition.

As part of observation process, the Executive should educate the family members and domestics to recognise fixed surveillance posts near the residence. Domestics can be of great help as they easily recognise strangers to the locality.

The matter should be confidentially reported to the higher police authorities.

## Planning

For meeting various contingencies, taking cue from the tips given in detail in the subsequent Chapters, detailed plans are to be prepared to cover all contingencies, escape routes, how to seek help in emergencies etc.

## Avoid Predictable Behaviour

We have seen that the miscreants plan their hits on the basis of predictable behaviour of the targets. Predictability is deadly. Since man is a creature of habit, unless special efforts are made, it will not be possible to get out of the routine. On the pretext of varying routine, one should not make the changes themselves in a routine manner. For example, it is not always necessary to go to office in the same car. A colleague can be asked to drop in and the executive can travel in that car, while his own car goes in a different direction. Routes can be varied. Hobbies can be rotated around. There are innumerable possibilities. Once unpredictability is seen, it becomes difficult for the miscreants to plan the kidnap.

## Create an Action Plan

The Executive should prepare an action plan to deal with his personal and family affairs in his absence. Bank accounts should be in joint names, nominations for all benefits like insurance etc. should be carefully checked and updated; a dossier consisting of all information should be prepared and kept ready as a will, a general power of attorney etc. A duplicate copy of all these should be available in the office or with a close friend.

## Mental Preparation

The executive should read the case histories of as many kidnap cases as possible and mentally work out how he would have reacted and behaved in those circumstances. Remember the adage: 'Wisemen learn from others' experience and not so wise (fools) learn from their own'

## Preparing for the Worst

Remember Murphy's Law. In spite of all these precautions, the Executive may be kidnapped. In that eventuality, survival will depend on individual's will power, capacity to take mature decisions and robust common sense. One should remember that a dead victim is a liability for the kidnapper and a bad business proposition. The kidnapper will not kill the hostage till he gets the ransom. Panic should be avoided. Kidnappers themselves will be under great stress. Any foolish behaviour on the part of the victim will invite reprisals. Escape should not be attempted without deep thinking and planning. In a new and unfamiliar location, one is likely to get trapped inviting more serious consequences. One should remain calm and be polite to the kidnappers and obey all their commands except those which are likely to place others in danger. Attempts should be made to build good human relations with captors or guards. The food offered should not be refused and to keep fit , physical exercises should be done within the given constraints. Mind should be kept occupied with positive thinking. One should not brood nor give out the names and particulars of favourite children and relatives. All neutral questions should be answered and care should be taken nor to give information, that may help further kidnappings. Never discuss politics or religion with the captors, lest they may be provoked. Be alert for any rescue attempts. Do not believe and accept what all the kidnappers say. They may try to break the victim psychologically. Dignity should be kept up. Do not beg for favours or cringe before kidnappers. One should have confidence in the family and the organisation; they must be doing their best to get the victim released. The process takes time. If there is belief in God, spend time in prayers.

Let us hope the eventuality of the executive becoming a kidnap victim never occurs. As Napoleon said "Trust in God and Keep the powder dry".

# 3

# Protective Arrangements at Home

I N TERMS OF SUCCESSFUL attempts at kidnapping, often, the miscreants have targeted the residences of potential victims. This is more so, when they could also 'pick up' some secondary targets like women and children to extract better ransom. It has been noted, when young children and women are the victims of kidnapping, there is greater success in extracting the ransom. It is possible to take sensible commonsense precautions to thwart the attempts at kidnapping of family members from home without converting the home a fortress. Here are some useful guidelines:

## Location

The Residence should be situated in a safe locality of the city. Avoid renting houses which are isolated and far from habitation. If possible, look for houses in upper middle class areas. There should be more than one approach road to reach the house. It should not be in the dead end of the road or in a *cul-de sac.* The house should have a compound wall and open spaces all round. If you already own a house, ensure that it has a compound wall and create open areas around. If there are vacant sites/plots adjacent to the house, ensure with the help of local police, that these open spaces are not frequented by undesirable characters.

## Perimeter Security

The compound wall is the first line of defence. It should be at least 7 feet high and it should not give scope for people to scale over and hide near it. While a 4 feet overhang to prevent people from scaling over is very useful, people do not like to have it, as it gives the appearance of a factory. Instead, broken glass can be fixed on the top of the wall all-round. Where possible, an alarm system should be installed. Inside, there should be a pathway all along the compound wall for the security guard or the guard dog to move around. There should be sturdy gates at the main entrance and a wicket gate for pedestrians to use. The gates should always be kept locked from inside and call bells are to be fitted at the gate for the visitors to announce themselves. The compound wall and the open areas around the house should be well lit in the night. The lights are to be operated from inside the house and they should be fixed in such a manner that it should not be possible for an intruder to interfere with them

## Open Area Around the House

Between the compound wall and the house, an open area should be created by clearing shrubs, bushes etc. No hedges and bushes are to be planted very close to the house or near the doors and windows. These provide an ideal place for the intruders to hide. The open area should be well lit during the night. If an alarm system is fixed in the compound wall, the lighting arrangement should be synchronised with it, to come on automatically, if there is a breach in the perimeter. It is also advisable to have an audio alarm to attract the attention of neighbours.

## Dogs

Guard dogs are very useful to patrol the perimeter during nights. These are to be trained properly by experts and should be let in the compound only during nights. They should be kept in the kennel during day time and except the handler who feeds them, no one should be allowed to pet them and become familiar with them. Many private security agencies hire out guard dogs. They are generally well trained and come with a handler, who is also a security guard. These dogs are trained to attack anyone unfamiliar to them. Therefore, there is need for the domestics and others to follow a well set routine. Once these dogs are let out in the compound, till morning, there should not be any movements in the area.

## Security Guards

Security guards are useful to man the gates and also to patrol the residence at night. If there are no company security guards, great care should be taken in employing private security guards. They should be hired only from a reputed firm and the protected person should take an active interest in supervising their work. The security firm should be instructed not to change their guards frequently and the changes are to be effected only after the protected person gives the consent. The guards should be prohibited from gossiping with domestics and leaving their posts frequently on some pretext. All essential facilities should be available in the guard post itself. They should be checked often in the night for alertness. There are inexpensive guard checking systems, which are tamper proof. They could be installed in different locations in the compound and the guard will be required to record his presence at various points. A simpler system is to make the guard blow the whistle at night at fixed intervals. While on rounds, he should also make sounds with his stick. Guards and dogs can become noisy in the nights while performing their duties. One should put up with this inconvenience.

## Doors and Windows

Most of the modern doors are ornamental and flimsy. They cannot withstand physical attack. It is therefore necessary to have sturdy doors and windows, which can resist an attack from outside. All doors and windows in the house are to be strengthened. Sliding doors are very vulnerable and can be easily tampered with. Special attention should be paid to them. At night, all the doors and windows are to be 'alarmed'. All glass surfaces are to be fitted with shatter proof film. Conventional vertical bolts, both at the top and bottom, will prevent these from being opened from outside.

At the main door, peep holes or lens should be fitted. There should be deadbolt and chain/bolt arrangement, and visitors are to be admitted only after proper identification. As a matter of policy, vendors and salesmen should not be allowed inside the house. When service personnel, like telephone mechanics or gas supply boys, visit the house, they should be let in only when the security guard or a domestic is present.

## Locks

Most of the standard locks can be opened by a semi-skilled person. Since the safety of the inmates depend on the locks holding firm the doors and windows, special attention should be paid to them .'Dead Bolt' systems supplemented with chain arrangement are ideal. Double cylinder locks which require two different keys for entry and exit are also very useful. Never leave the house keys outside the house by hiding them in a flower bed or pot. Nor, part with house keys to anyone. It takes only a few minutes to duplicate them.

## Hinges

Often the hinges of doors and windows are overlooked. In most places, one will find the hinges on the outside of the door. It will be a child's play to remove the hinge pin and bodily lift the doors with the locks. Hinges should be mounted inside. The pin should be welded or a screw arrangement should be made to prevent the pin from being prised out.

## Curtains

Have heavy curtains and draw them during the night. Even during day time, open the curtains only in the areas being used.

## Lighting

It is important to have a master switch in your bedroom, which can switch on all interior lights at the same time. External lights should face away from the house. There should be a separate arrangement for keeping the security lights on, in case of power failure or sabotage.

## Keeping a Dog Inside the House

A good watch dog is an efficient burglar alarm. Even when some one rings the door bell, the dog will indicate by its barking and behaviour, whether the person at the door is a stranger or a known person. A big dog is preferable. Dogs may not neutralise intruders, but they give advance warning that a suspicious and unwelcome being is inside the house. Unlike the dogs used for patrolling the compound, the dog inside the house stays with the family wherever they may be at a particular point of time. House dogs should not be hired from outside. A well trained pup should be bought and trained by the executive. They can also be used as escort, when children are sent out alone. A house dog should not be admonished, if it barks or growls at the visitors.

## Alarms and Warning Devices

There are many alarm and warning systems in the market. Take the help of the Security Officer of the firm or ask for a demonstration to satisfy that the system selected suits the actual needs. Alarms are to be installed by the specialists and are to be serviced regularly. Alarm systems have the annoying habit of going off due to various reasons. These are erroneously described as 'False Alarms'. As a matter of fact, there is no such thing as a false alarm; there are only non-actionable alarms. Alarms are not human beings, they only indicate that some thing is wrong. If possible, link the alarm system to the local police station.

## Communications

Before attacking a residence, miscreants often snap the telephone lines to prevent the victims from contacting others for help. To a great extent, cellular phones have solved this problem. There should be a cellular phone available in the nights with the line in domestic or someone, who sleeps on the same premises away from the main family. There should be a call bell or electronic call bell system with them or with the nighbours and a signal should be pre-arranged to indicate emergencies. As soon as this signal is given, the recipient should telephone the police and seek help.

## Domestic Servants

They should be selected and hired with great care. References are to be checked and verified. Never snatch domestic servants from others. Domestics can be very useful in locating surveillance around the house; they can also provide local intelligence. Treat them well. Bad treatment of domestic servants breed disloyalty in them and makes them prone for subversion. Never allow domestics to accommodate their friends and relatives in the servant quarters.

## Firearm in the House

If there is a firearm, keep it in good working order and in an accessible place for emergencies. Be familiar with its operations and how to use it in an emergency. Also teach one or two adult members, how to use it. More than Revolvers and Pistols, Pump Action Shot guns are very useful for protection. They maim and stop the intruders without killing them.

## Safe Havens

It is likely that the intruders have already entered the house. Entire family should know that they should retreat to the pre-selected safe haven. A safe haven is a specially selected room in the house which can be closed and will not allow access to outsiders. It will have additional locking arrangements with sturdy doors. It will have an emergency First Aid Kit, Drinking Water, Cellular Telephone, Fire Extinguisher and the Fire Arm.

## Fire Extinguishers

All rooms in the house should have portable Fire Extinguishers and Smoke Alarms.

**Telephones**

Are often used to blackmail or threaten the inmates, to gather information about the whereabouts of the intended victim, and to check the presence of people in the house. Family members and the Secretaries are to be trained to deal with these effectively.

To determine how good is the present security of a residence, the checklist given below may be used to evaluate the actual conditions. This checklist is only illustrative. Additions are to be made to meet specific requirements of the environment.

## Home Security Checklist

**Location**

Is it satisfactory? Are there more than one approach? Can one get away from the Residence in case of an attack? Are the approaches well lit during nights? Are there vacant plots being frequented by undesirable persons? Are police aware of the presence of these elements? Have they been informed?

## Perimeter Wall

Are there any gaps in the wall? Can one climb the wall easily? Is there a pathway inside the compound wall for the Security Guard and the Dog to patrol?

## Open Space Around the House

Is there sufficient open space around the Building? Have bushes and shrubs been cleared? Are there any hedges and bushes near the doors and windows which can enable an intruder to hide in them?

## Lighting

Are the grounds and perimeter wall lit during the night? Is it possible for an intruder to tamper with the lights? Is there an arrangement to switch on all interior lights from the master bedroom?

## Garage

Is it connected with the main house? Can one enter the car from inside the house? Is the garage always kept locked? Can the garage doors be opened from outside without a Key?

## Doors and Windows

Are they strong to withstand attack from outside? Are the locks tamper proof? Have the glasses on the windows and doors shatter proof film? Are the doors always kept locked?

## Peephole

Is there a Peephole or a viewing lens on the main door? Is there a dead bolt and chain arrangement on the main door?

## Dogs

Are the patrolling and house dogs carefully selected and trained?

## Communications

Do you have alternate arrangements to deal with the situation, if the telephone lines are snapped or sabotaged? Is there a signal between master bed room and the servant quarters and the neighbours to alert them in case of danger?

## Fire Extinguishers/Smoke Alarms

Are they available in every room and are in working order?

## Firearm

Is it kept in a place where it can be reached in an emergency? Are you familiar with the use of the weapon? Have you trained one or two members of your household how to use the weapon in an emergency or in case you become disabled?

## Domestic Servants

Have you taken precautions to check their antecedents with the police or with the referees? Are you treating them with kindness? Are they loyal?

## Safe Havens

Have you selected a suitable room and equipped it to serve as a Safe Haven in times of emergencies?

## Family Members

Have they been briefed to implement all the security instructions and not to accept parcels, packets etc. from unknown persons and not to allow strangers inside the house? Do they know how to react when they receive a telephone call about your being in trouble and what positive steps are to be taken by them?

## When You are Away

Have you listed out precautions to be taken when you are

away from the house on vacation and the house remains locked?

**Telephones**

Do your family members know what to do when they are querried about your movements and other details or when they receive large number of wrong calls?

# 4

# Security of Office and Workplace

ATTACKS ON EXECUTIVES in offices very rarely occur. However, many kidnappings of Executives have taken place from the place of work. Often, these have taken place at the time when the Executive alighted from his car to enter the office premises or at the time when he left the office. Assuming that the Executive has tightened the security arrangements at the residence and during the road journeys, the miscreants will turn their attention to the workplace. They will always strike at the weakest point in the security arrangements. Often the executive is lulled into inaction from the fact that large number of people work in the office and they afford a sort of shield from attacks. Basic aim of all security arrangements in the office is to keep out people who are likely to cause harm to the plant, workers and the executive. The steps suggested here will benefit everyone, while ensuring the safety of the executive.

According to a security expert, "The strongest castle walls are not proof against the traitor within". Thus efficacy of the system will depend on the trustworthiness of the staff. A dedicated and loyal staff, trained to be alert to the security threats, can improve the overall security situation in the office. They are the people who can give advance warning about things that are amiss. Every office has a security wing, however rudimentary and inefficient it may be. One can build on this existing frame, a good security system. Some guidelines are below:

## Security Audit

The first step is to engage a security consultant to inspect the office and carry out the security audit. He will report on the strengths and weaknesses of the existing arrangements. After careful scrutiny of this report and after discussions with the Security Officer, various recommendations can be prioritised for implementation.

## Office Location

It is necessary to locate the office in a safe locality. Unlike the residence, the busier the area it is better from security angle. Business centres in the heart of the city are patrolled by the Police regularly and often a mobile Radio-van is stationed in those locations. If the Company is renting out space for the first time, it is better to take space for offices in the upper floors. Try to avoid renting premises next to Universities, Colleges, Political Party Offices and such kind. You are likely to become the target of demonstrations against these targets and in the resulting vandalism, your property and assets may be damaged.

## Perimeter Security

Office security begins at the perimeter. Natural and structural barriers like Fences, Drop barriers, Gates, etc. provide the first obstacle for the mischief monger. Speed breakers near the main gate will prevent speeding vehicles gate crashing. All personnel and vehicles entering through the main gate are to be checked. In disturbed areas, no vehicle should be allowed to be parked near the main building to prevent damage from car bombs. All possible ways providing entry into the building should be guarded. At night, the building should be well lit to deter intruders from lurking in the shadows. Auxiliary power units for security lighting should be provided for.

## Access Control

Without disturbing the normal functioning of the office, an efficient access control system should be enforced. All personnel, irrespective of their status in the office should wear and prominently display their I.D.Cards. Visitors, after proper screening should be issued with Visitors badges valid for only a particular section of the building and they should be escorted in and out by the security personnel. It is advisable for visitors seeking interviews with top executives, without prior appointment, are seen by junior personnel at the first instance and after satisfying about their genuineness, they could be taken to senior executives.

## Checking of Mail and Parcels

All incoming mail should be screened with the help of a Letter Bomb Detector. Parcels are to be x-rayed. Security guards should be advised not to accept any parcels and packets meant for senior executives and pass them on without inspection and check. Details of how to deal with threats from explosives and methods to deal with them are given in Chapter XI.

## Maintenance Staff

Maintenance staff, who normally work in the nights for cleaning and janitorial chores are to be properly screened and if possible, they should work under the supervision of the security personnel. Security guards should be present with them, when they clean the rooms of top executives.

## Telephone Security

Secretaries and personal staff are to be briefed not to give out information about the movement and personal particulars of the top executives on the phone. They should be familiarised and practiced to deal with Bomb Threats.

## Security Alarms

The office should have a well conceived and effective security alarm systems preferably linked with the Police Control Room.

## Visitor Control

No visitor should be allowed to go into the Top Executive's room without being vetted by the Secretary. Where the threats are acute, a Metal Detector can be placed at the entrance of the Secretary's room. This can be suitably camouflaged. There should be system of warning buttons. If the Secretary suspects the bonafides of the visitor, she should activate the warning button, and the chief security officer, who should always be in plainclothes, can come into the Secretary's room and take charge of the situation. The access to the Executive's room from the Secretary's room should have a strong door with a latch arrangement, which can be released either by the Secretary or by the Executive only. This will prevent people from rushing into the room.

## Special Precautions for Executive's Protection

**1. Alighting point**

As soon as the security receives the intimation that the Executive had left the residence and on his way to the office, they should carefully scout the surrounding areas and remove any truck or car with passengers parked on the approach road. They should keep the alighting point clear of people and vehicles. As the executive gets down from the car, they should provide him a physical shield and escort him in to the office.

**2. Lift**

At the time of arrival, the lift should be kept ready and empty.

The executive should be directly taken to his chambers.

### 3. Panic Button

Top Executives should be provided with a 'Personal Distress Alarm' system commonly known as 'Panic Button'. In case, he expects rough behaviour or assault or threat from the visitor, he should quietly press this button. This button will immediately alert the Security officer and his staff.

### 4. Emergency Exit

An emergency exit should be available in the Private Toilet, which should be part of the office room. This toilet should have a strong door with dead bolt arrangement. In case of trouble, the executive can get into the toilet and bolt himself. Normal and cellular telephones should be available inside the toilet to summon help. There should be an exit door, which should allow the executive to leave unobtrusively.

### 5. Use of Weapons

Under no circumstances the Executive should resort to the use of Firearm. The miscreant would have come well prepared and it is difficult to take him on. Prudence should be the better part of valour.

### 6. Bullet Proof Brief Case/Writing Pad

Bullet proof brief cases and table writing pads are now available in different sizes and options. These are handy to protect oneself from sudden attack with small weapons. These can be provided to Top Executives.

### 7. Attack Dogs

In difficult areas, attack dogs could be used by the Executives. These well trained dogs will accompany the Executive from the residence to office and will remain in the office room. On a signal from the master, it will attack any intruder. These dogs are very effective, provided they have been properly trained and handled carefully.

To determine how good are the security arrangements at the office, the checklist given below may be used to double check the existing arrangements. The list is only illustrative.

## Physical Security Checklist for Offices

### 1. Security Audit

When was one carried out? Have all the suggestions been implemented? If the previous Security Audit was done over three years ago, get a fresh one done.

### 2. Responsibility for Physical Security

Who is responsible for Physical Security of the Office premises? Does he has sufficient administrative authority to implement security programmes? Does he report to the Chief Executive once a week, as a matter of routine?

### 3. Perimeter Security

Is the perimeter security arrangements satisfactory? Are there any gaps or deficiencies?

### 4. Access Control

**Are they well defined with clear cut responsibility? How access control is enforced?**

### 5. Main Entrance

(*a*) Who is manning the main entrance? Can anyone enter without his knowledge? Are the personnel manning the entry point have a clear view of those approaching them?
(*b*) Can anyone force his way through, disregarding the person manning the entrance?
(*c*) Is there any device for the personnel at the main entrance to raise an alarm in the event of a forced entry?

(*d*) Are there separate entrances for the regular employees, visitors and contract labour?
(*e*) Who Checks the I.D.Cards and how?
(*f*) Is there an ante-room for visitors?

**6**. How postal deliveries are handled? Are there any arrangements for screening the mail and parcels?

**7**. What is the system for admitting maintenance people, telephone mechanics, electricians etc.?

**8**. Are the reception staff familiar with the Fire drill, and know what to do in case of Fire, Bomb Threats etc.?

**9**. Are back up personnel available in case of rush of visitors?

## Security Measures

1. Is there a Door Frame Metal Detector at the main entrance and the entrance to the office of the top executive?
2. Is there a Letter Bomb Detector?
3. Is there an x-ray system to screen parcels and Packages?
4. Is there an ante-room to do physical check and frisking if it becomes necessary?
5. Are there Hand held Metal Detectors?
6. Are Visitors' belongings carefully stored at the reception and acknowledgments issued?
7. Are visitors being registered regularly and passes are issued and collected from them and accounted for every day? Are visitors being escorted by security personnel into the office?
8. How passes are issued and checked in respect of contract and casual labour?
9. Are permanent passes/I.D. Cards being displayed by the staff and are checked?
10. Is there a system of Key Control?
11. Are principles of documentary security being enforced?
12. How often the Telephones, FAX machines are being checked by experts to prevent eaves dropping?

13. Are Top Level meetings held in secure halls?
14. Is disposal of waste paper, carbons, cartridges, floppies being done properly?
15. During lunch and Coffee breaks, does anyone remain in the hall to take care of the documents?
16. Are the Fire Drills and Evacuation drills being followed and practiced regularly?
17. Is the scheme for dealing with Bomb Threats available? Are staff familiar with that? How Often rehearsed?
18. Are the Drills for the protection of Executives being followed carefully and faithfully?
19. How often the security arrangements are tested and with what result?

# 5

# Meeting Threats During Road Journeys

ALL OVER THE WORLD, majority of the kidnappings have taken place while the business executive was travelling by car either from Home to his office or on the return journey and on some occasions while he was proceeding to, or returning from, a social function. Most of these incidents have taken place few hundred yards from the home. Travelling by car has become a necessity for the busy executive. While the office and often the home, have fool proof security, the car becomes very vulnerable due to restricted scope for making security arrangements.

It is interesting to note that kidnaps take place nearer home for the simple reason, because most Executives believe in punctuality-particularly in the mornings and the departure time is almost constant; as the executive leaves his home, he has a very few options to change the route; people tend to feel very protected in a car, and often get immersed in newspapers or paper work and do not pay attention to the surroundings; most of the Executives travel alone in the car; and finally the car of the executive is easy to identify. Inspite of these, it is easy to defeat the kidnappers, if an Executive follows some simple preventive steps.

## Preventive Measures

### (a) Foil Target Selection

A kidnapper selects his target carefully. He wishes to ensure that his efforts yield a good return. He looks for the executive with wealth signified by lavish life style and ostentation. He also looks for an Executive, who has a set and predictable pattern of activities. Human being is a creature of habit. He likes to wear often the same type of dress; likes to reserve the same table in hotels; and likes to follow a well set routine. He also likes to show off his wealth and possessions. He likes to be admired and also envied. These traits are carefully observed by a kidnapper and he takes these into account while making his plans. If a potential victim could avoid ostentation and get over the urge to be predictable and frequently changes his routine, it will cause problems for the kidnapper in planning the kidnapping. He is likely to avoid this unpredictable target and select someone whose kidnapping is easy to organise.

**(b) Defeating Surveillance**

Kidnapping is a meticulously planned and professionally executed operation. Planning is the essence of success. Surveillance is resorted to, for collection of necessary information about the activities of the victim and to grab him at the time and place when he will be very vulnerable. The kidnapper organises surveillance to observe the movements of the victim at the time of departure from home or office; while he is in a vehicle; and on the move. This is done with the help of vehicles with observers, which take position near the residence of the victim or by placing persons as watchers near the targeted area. Domestics like gardeners, drivers etc. are encouraged to gossip and information obtained about the habits of the target. Often, kidnappers photograph the activities of the victim at the time of departure. Once the vehicle is on the move, it is followed closely and the route, traffic intersections, traffic signals, stretches of road with no or little traffic are carefully noted. This is done over a long period of time to pinpoint the pattern in the movements of the potential victim and to locate the ideal place for carrying out the abduction and to whisk away the victim.

It is not very difficult to locate surveillance. Except for the highly trained professionals, other people indulging in surveillance can be easily spotted. All of us observe unconsciously our surroundings and if there is a change, we feel it. As one drives for work, he knows exactly at what point he will see the elderly gentleman taking his dog for a walk or the mother taking her daughter to the school bus 'pick up point'. He also observes which of the shops are open and the state of business carried on. These things get registered automatically without any effort. If one is conscious of changes in the surroundings, one can easily detect the surveillance. Points to be observed are: Unknown vehicles parked near the residence or near the office with people sitting in them; People, who do not belong to the area, standing, walking, or sitting in cars near the residence or office; while driving, looking into the rear view mirror to notice any vehicle persistently following; while entering the office/workplace, noting the vehicles that drive past and return to the same spot after a few minutes. In other words, a conscious effort to keep note of unusual sightings and activities around oneself. A memo-corder or a small portable tape recorder should be available in the car and unusual observations can be recorded as one drives along. In respect of vehicles, the Make, Model, Year, Colour, Registration number, any special features and the number and type of the people in it can be described and recorded. This information can be transferred into a log and if a pattern is discernible, the matter can be reported to the police. It is also necessary to brief and train the chauffer to observe unusual happenings. Domestic help could also be briefed to notice presence of unusual activities around the residence.

One could also test the efficacy and the impact of these instructions on the domestics/chauffer by deploying simulated surveillance without their knowledge and finding out whether the surveillance has been noticed.

### (c) Route variation

It is possible to vary the route in a systematic manner. With the assistance of the road map, several alternative routes can be worked out between the residence and the office. Each route is assigned a number and the chauffer is told to take a particular numbered route for the journey. This can be varied both for the onward and return journey. No doubt, some of the routes will be longer and may take a little extra time. Care however should be taken to plan the routes in busy areas and not in isolated patches.

### (d) Locating Vulnerable areas

One should carefully study the area around the residence and office, and locate areas where it will be easy to stop the car and abduct the person. This could be a traffic signal near the residence, an approach road to the office or the Airport etc. These vulnerable areas cannot be avoided but one can plan to spend the least possible time in these areas and mentally prepare a plan to come out of the area in case of an ambush. One should carefully scan the area to locate safe places nearby where one can seek refuge in times of danger. These places will be those frequented by members of the public like Police Stations, Fire Stations, Hospitals, Shopping arcades and Protected areas like Military establishments. The kidnappers are not likely to follow the victim into these areas once he escapes from their trap. Having located these safe places, one should become proficient about the route and short cuts to reach them quickly.

### (e) Precautions while travelling

Keep all the car doors locked from inside. If you are travelling alone, travel in the front seat next to the driver. Have a mobile phone or a wireless set. Inform the destination as you are leaving, about your departure and the expected time of arrival. In case you change your plans enroute to attend to some urgent business, immediately inform the destination. In case you do not arrive at the destination at the expected time or within a reasonable time, an all out search for you should be launched and the police should be informed.

**(f) The Chauffer**

Sufficient care should be taken to verify the background and antecedents of the Chauffer. Once satisfied, he should be trained to take the required precautions to prevent an ambush or abduction. Where training facilities are available, he should be trained in defensive driving and counter-ambush drill. He should be medically examined at least once a year for his general health, reflexes and eyesight.

**(g) Warning Systems**

To attract attention in case of trouble, fit in the car a siren, which could be activated both from the driver's seat and the passenger cabin. Both the chauffer and the Executive should develop some signals to communicate to one another in case they locate trouble.

**(h) Anti-Tamper Warning Systems**

It is necessary to fit in the vehicle, anti-tamper warning systems, so that when the car is ever interfered with, the occupants can notice the same fact before entering the vehicle.

**(i) Trauma Kit**

The vehicle should have a trauma kit specially designed to deal with gunshot injuries, burns, stab wounds, and heart failure. This kit should be available in the passenger cabin and should not be locked in the trunk.

## How to Select A Good Vehicle to Meet Threats to Personal Security

When dealing with potential threats, the Executive should be careful in selecting a good car which will aid in a quick getaway in times of crisis. Following options should be demanded and catered for:

1. Get the maximum powerful engine that the vehicle can support.
2. Door locks should be below surface types and capable of being opened through remote control from a distance.
3. Trunk, Hood and Petrol Tank should have locking arrangements which can be operated only from inside the car.
4. The car should have Dual side mirrors with remote control.
5. Power steering with special provisions to withstand rough steering.
6. Power disc brakes.
7. Steel belted radial Tyres.
8. Air conditioning.
9. Heavy duty suspension.
10. Siren or Fog horn.
11. High intensity head and reversing lights.
12. Communication systems.
13. Grill mounted flasher lights to attract attention.
14. Concealed external microphones to communicate with the people outside the vehicle.

## Bullet Proof Vehicles

Bullet Proof Vehicles or Armoured cars are nowadays becoming very common. These are cars fitted with armour in a concealed manner and bullet resistant glass and look like any other car of the same model without attracting attention. These are custom built. These are also available in India.

The normal procedure for acquiring the bullet proof car, is for the protected person to select a vehicle of his choice and give it to the specialist firm for armouring. As the protected person or his firm has to give the specifications, it will be useful to know the following finer points.

***Selection of the Vehicle***: Always select the type of the vehicle that is commonly in use in the country. Since the vehicle has to carry extra weight of the armour and the glass, it should be a sturdy one and capable of best performance under strain. The points earlier stressed on selecting a good vehicle should be kept in mind.

***Level of Protection***: The customer has to indicate the level of protection he needs. These have been standardised in the United States and are now universally accepted. These are classified as Levels of Protection II, III and IV. Performance criteria are given below:

***Level II*** : Capable of stopping a 9mm bullet fired from a Pistol or Revolver at close quarters and is also capable of stopping a .357 magnum bullet.

***Level III*** : In addition to the above, can also stop a 44 magnum, 12 gauge ball shot, and .30 caliber carbine bullets.

***Level IV*** : In addition to the above, also stops heavy 30.06 NATO ball ammunition.

At this level, the vehicle will be capable of withstanding bullets travelling at 2400 ft/per second. It should be remembered that there are many Army weapons, which easily surpass this velocity. There are also special ammunition, known as armour piercing ammunition. Thus, the bullet proof car can only give protection against weapons commonly encountered.

***Bullet Resistant Glass***: For the bullet proof car, all glass surfaces are replaced with bullet resistant glasses. These are quite thick and weigh a lot. If bullets are continuously fired at the same spot, it is possible to pierce them. They do not break but the pieces are held together. Often, they come in a sandwich pattern. Even if the outer layer is broken, the inner layer holds fast.

***Armouring Materials***: In the same vehicle, for different areas, different materials are used. They could be B.P.Steel plates, Toughened Aluminum alloy: Ceramic plates, Kevlar fabrics etc.

***Performance Expectations*** : A bullet proof car should be capable of

(*a*) Absorbing a sudden attack from a fire arm, withstand repeated hits, return the fire and also have communication facilities to call for help.

(*b*) Absorb the initial attack and also break through the ambush.

***Armouring of the Vehicle***: It is not only the passenger cabin, but also the doors, windows, rear of the passenger seats, radiator, fuel tank, roof and the floor etc. are to be armoured. It should be realised that the bullet requires only a small area to penetrate the vehicle. Kidnappers are likely to use automatic weapons and spray the vehicle with bullets. No one can be sure which area will be hit.

***Additional Requirement for the Bullet Proof car :***

1. *Chassis* : Should be capable of withstanding the additional weight.
2. *Suspension and Springs* : Are to be strengthened to perform with extra load.
3. *Engine* : to be powerful and covered with armour.
4. *Tyres* : Should be radial steel belted and have run flat system on them.
5. *Steering* : Heavy duty power steering which can withstand the quick steering maneuvers needed in an emergency.
6. *Brakes* : Power brakes which can stop the vehicle instantly.
7. *Communications* : The vehicle should have radio-telephone or wireless to communicate with outside world in the event of an ambush.
8. *Mirrors* : Remote controlled rear view and side mirrors, capable of 360 degree observation from within the car.
9. *Horn* : Loud and powerful to attract attention.
10. *Public Address System* : The occupants should be able to talk to people outside the vehicle without opening the doors.
11. *Clear Glass* : There should be no distortion in the image when seen through the Bullet Proof glasses.
12. *Tool Kit* : A tool kit should be available inside the car to enable the occupants to free themselves in case they are trapped inside the car.
13. *Anti-skid Balancing* : Adjustments in the car are to be made to prevent skidding.

## Precautions while Buying Bullet Proof Cars

Bullet proof cars are very expensive. Since the life of the protected person depends on the performance of the armouring done, great care and attention should be paid at all stages. In the first place, only reputed firms should be selected for armouring. Full list of their clients should be obtained and the performance of cars should be checked with them. Quality control should be ensured at all stages of manufacture. The car should be tested at all stages for performance. Lastly, an agreement for future servicing should be secured.

## Driver of the Bullet Proof Car

The efficacy of the bullet proof car is directly dependent on the professional competence of the driver. It is an unusually heavy vehicle and will demand exacting professional skills to drive it at high speeds, to take turns and to negotiate traffic in congested areas. Therefore, the driver should be specially trained to handle the car. The car can be used as a weapon of offence in emergencies and the driver should also know defencive driving to avoid surveillance and to get out of traps and ambushes.

## Some Guidelines for Safe Travel

1. Never enter your vehicle without carrying out a walk around inspection.
2. Observe the surroundings for any car which is ready to follow you.
3. Drive with all doors locked from inside and windows rolled up.
4. Do not give lift to strangers, particularly attractive women with a large hand bag.
5. Keep good distance between the cars in front and rear to avoid getting boxed-in.

6. Keep a watch on cars, motor cycles etc. keeping pace with you. In two wheelers, watch the pillion rider, on the rear view mirror, carefully for any overt action.
7. Intersections, Railway level crossings and Traffic lights are potential trouble spots. Keep alert.
8. If followed, do not panic. Just drive into a crowded location preferably a police station, public administration building, military establishment so on. If more people are around, there are less chances of trouble coming your way.
9. Invite police attention by doing something wrong or creating traffic violations. Once you are in the company of police, no harm is likely.
10. Speed is only a temporary escape. Do not drive in panic into unknown areas. You are likely to be trapped.
11. Do not stop at accidents, diversions etc. If you see one ahead, reverse your direction of travel and take a different route.
12. If a car blocks your way, drive with full speed and hit the car at the tail portion. When the blocking car turns on impact, make your getaway.
13. If the kidnappers shoot at your Tyres and damage them, continue driving. The Tyres and rim may get damaged and may also damage the road surface, but you can drive safely up to 7/8 kilometers. Similarly, a damaged radiator, broken fan belt etc. should not deter you from continuing to drive. The engine may get damaged but your life will be safe.
14. Even if you have a weapon with you, do not stop to engage the kidnappers in a gun battle. They are professionals and they can beat you any time. Use the weapon only as a last resort.

## Explosives in Cars

Miscreants place explosives in cars either to kill the person driving the car or to cause harm to the facility into which the car would be driven in or to cause harm to the people who will be nearer the car at the time of explosion. Planting an explosive in a car is easy but the miscreant would need time for that. The first principle to save oneself from this danger is to never leave the car alone and unlocked. Even while in the garage, the car should be kept locked and the garage should be locked. Second precaution is never to enter the parked car without carrying out a visual inspection of the car by walking around the car. Points to be noted are: whether there are any unidentified packages, parcels etc. in the car; are there any wires protruding from the dash board; from under the floor; or has the hood been tampered with. The exhaust pipe is the favourite place for hiding explosives. Therefore during inspection, the exhaust pipe, wheel wells etc. are to be checked for any caked mud, unusual projections etc. As already stated, a silent anti-tamper alarm should be fixed in the car and it should give an indication of tampering during the inspection from outside. If the threat level is high, it will be useful to have mirrors which could be used to check the under carriage. Most of the explosives are set to explode when the engine is started. It is better to start the engine from outside using a remote control and idle the engine for a few seconds. Similarly, it would be wise to enter the car from the passenger side than from the driver's side. All cars entering a protected facility should be checked for explosives.

## Remember

Kidnapping a targeted individual while on the move is a serious enterprise. Lot of thinking and planning goes into its execution. Calm and calculated response alone can defeat the attempt at kidnapping. It is a battle of wits. One with superior intelligence succeeds. So never lose your cool. When faced with kidnapping threat while on the move, remember that you are alone and your life depends on your ability to act decisively and calmly. Do not panic nor exhibit bravado. Your aim should be to get out of the trouble spot as quickly as possible. Follow the simple steps outlined. If you have the services of a security professional, consult him and act on his advice regarding precautions to be taken. Please remember that the vehicle does not assure any safety inspite of its sturdy looks. It is your intelligence and preventive actions that will save you from becoming a kidnap victim.

# 6

# Protection During Air and Foreign Travel

Business executives should take due precautions during their air journeys and foreign tours. Unless they are well known internationally as very rich and wealthy, it will be stretching one's imagination to the realms of fancy, to conceive of local miscreants, planning to attack them while in a commercial aircraft or on foreign soil. However, often the Executives get into difficulties for the simple reason that they were in the wrong place at the wrong time. Elementary precautions would ensure that, at least one is not in the wrong place. Careful planning can also avoid the wrong time.

## Air Travel

Most important aspects of security that should concern an air traveller are:

1. Protection against gunmen or bombers in the check-in area to which general public has access. Recall what happened in Rome and Vienna airports in 1985.
2. Attempts to plant guns or explosives in the baggage of gullible passengers. In April 1986, a 'good Samaritan' miscreant on the pretext of helping a pregnant lady, tried to plant offensive items in her cabin baggage on an El Al aircraft in Heathrow Airport.
3. A passenger leaving an explosive in the registered baggage and later not joining the flight. Recall the case of Air

India 747 blown up over the Atlantic in June 1985.

4. A miscreant leaving a hand baggage on board with explosives during transit and not reboarding the Aircraft. Recall the incident concerning TWA flight from Rome to Athens in April 1986.

Airport security is the concern of the State authorities. Every human system is bound to fail when things become too monotonous and routine. Millions of air passengers fly all over the world and safely complete their journey. Yet, Hijackings do take place inspite of the security arrangements at the airports. In all cases, the disaster was traced to human failure. A little awareness among the passengers to ensure that there is no laxity in the implementation of these security precautions, will go a long way in ensuring cent per cent safety. What should an Executive do to ensure his own safety during Air travels? Follow the guidelines given below:

## Guidelines

1. Travel Plans: are to be kept confidential in the organisation on 'Need to know Basis'.
2. Air Ticket Bookings: should be done with a discreet travel agent and the tickets should be kept as confidential documents. Travel by well known Air Carriers only. Do not be tempted by discounts.
3. Departure: reach the Airport ahead of time. Do not avail of the facilities offered in Executive Lounges or Exclusive Clubs at the Airport, located in areas open to general public. Check in and proceed through security checks and relax in the' sterile ' area.'
4. VIP Status: Do not display your VIP status with special tags, expensive brief cases etc. and receive and transmit your calls on the Cellular Phone in a discreet corner.
5. Avoid inquisitive passengers or those trying to be too friendly and try information about your business at the destination.
6. Do not stay with abandoned luggages. If possible, report

the matter to airport security.

7. During transit, watch out for the neighbour leaving his baggage and not rejoining the flight. Inform cabin crew.
8. Prefer a window seat.
9. Destination: Ensure your reception is common place. Ask someone known to you to meet you at the airport. Otherwise, take a taxi from the line and reach your destination. Preferably, travel in the Hotel Coach or Airlines coach to reach the city. Never get into a vehicle, where an unknown person welcomes you. He should bring a letter of introduction from your host.
10. Do not allow the taxi to pick up passengers on the way.
11. If your luggage is not bulky, keep it with you in the rear seat.
12. Never part with your brief case. Be prepared for snatchers.
13. Keep local currency in small denominations with you. Never open your brief case in front of the taxi driver to give him the fare nor leave your luggage in the car to change your travellers' cheques or currency. Do these in the Airport itself.
14. Keep your Travel documents in the inside pocket of your Jacket. In a new place, they are the most valuable piece of evidence to establish your identity.

## Hijacking

Hijackings have come to stay. In case an Executive's Aircraft becomes a victim of hijacking, one should keep the following in mind.

1. The first few minutes of Hijackings are very crucial. The miscreants will be highly excited and will be prone to use violence at the least provocation to establish their mastery over the passengers. Passengers will react to the event either in disbelief, anger or aggression. Hysteria may develop. On these occasions, keep your cool. Remain as unobtrusive as possible. Do not fall a victim to the impulse of aggression

2. The hijacker is not a Traffic cop trying to give you a ticket. Do not volunteer unnecessary personal information, particularly about your status and position in the company nor family details. More you try to impress him, the more valuable you become to him as a bargain token. Pretend that you are too shocked to be coherent and answer as far as possible in mono syllables.
3. Do not crack jokes or try to show the miscreants in a bad light. Their discomfiture will land you in trouble. This is one occasion, where being smart is not good.
4. Try to calm your neighbours, if they become hysterical.
5. In case of a shooting, duck and lie low.
6. The ordeal may last for quite some time. So, be mentally prepared. Try to do some isometric exercises and breathing exercises from the sitting position and keep the mind occupied with mental games.
7. Do not make any move that is likely to be misunderstood by the kidnappers.
8. If you have a medical problem, explain that in simple terms to the miscreants.
9. Keep your dignity. Never breakdown nor beg for favours.
10. Remember. Hijackers normally do not kill the passengers. They wish to use them as pawns or levers for negotiation with the authorities. While the final outcome is uncertain, in majority of the hijackings, most of the passengers came out unhurt.
11. In case the plane is stormed by the special forces, duck and remain at a low level. Do not stand up. The Special Forces have only a few seconds to succeed in their mission. They will shoot everything that moves. Never offer yourself as a target. Nor do they need your cheering. Wait till the operation is over and the commander announces that the Hijacking has been terminated.
12. Offer your services to the Special Forces to evacuate old and infirm, ladies and children first.

## Precautions for Executive Aircraft

While an executive jet adds to the convenience and prestige, it has many limitations. It is true that the fear of highjacking is eliminated and you can choose the company you want. Compared to commercial Airliners, the Executive jets receive very little or no attention from the Airport security authorities. Following precautions are essential.

1. Get a Security consultant to provide a security drill for the Aircraft crew while at the base and on tour.
2. Aircraft should be secured carefully and should be checked often. Usually, the Executive Aircrafts are parked in isolated places and it is easy for a miscreant to sabotage or place an explosive.
3. Aircraft should be serviced in the presence of the Air crew.
4. While parked, special self-destruct seals are to be used to cover the aircraft's entrances, ports and other vital parts, to detect tampering.
5. The Crew should carry out a preflight anti-sabotage inspection well before departure.
6. All luggage going on board should be identified. No unaccompanied baggage should be taken on board and no hitch hikers should be allowed.
7. Request Airport security to help in carrying out standard drills for passenger checks.
8. In the nights, the parking area should be well lit.
9. Establish a communication drill for the air crew to be contacted if something goes amiss. Similarly, a drill for an emergency take off should be available. Air crew should be in touch with the Executive all the time.
10. If the aircraft has an alarm system, the Airport authorities should be briefed about it to enable them to react appropriately. They should know how to reach the crew in an emergency.
11. It is useful to train one of your staff on liaison duties connected with the protection of the aircraft.

## Precautions During Foreign Travel

1. Make a thorough study of the country to be visited and the present state of the law and order situation. Do not visit a country, when internal turmoil is on. Travel only when you must.
2. Itinerary should be carefully drawn up in consultation with the people who had been there before, like someone from the Foreign Service who had stayed in the country for some time. Their knowledge about local customs, traditions, prejudices etc. will be invaluable.
3. In respect of high profile and high-risk executives, advance publicity of the programme and other details should not be given.
4. Personal documents like Passports, I.D.Cards, Driving license etc. should be photocopied and one set should be available separately in the luggage. In other words, if the original is lost these will become useful to obtain duplicates. For the same reason, do not keep all the Travellers cheques together in one place. Passport, I.D.Card, Credit Cards etc. should always be carried in person. Never leave these in the Hotel Room.
5. Air travel precautions and departure and arrival precautions have been already enumerated in the previous paragraphs. They should be followed faithfully.
6. Before leaving the country, get to know and memorise in the concerned foreign language the equivalent of important words like, Fire, Police, Doctor, Help, Water etc.
7. Keep some amount of foreign currency in small denominations to meet the expenditure on arrival like paying the Taxi Fare, tipping the Bell Captain, making a local call etc.
8. Keep in your Wallet the telephone numbers of the important contacts in the country visited.
9. Carry extra Passport size Photographs. These will be needed to make documentation.

10. Check into a well reputed Hotel, even if it is slightly expensive.
11. Avoid taking ground floor rooms.
12. Always keep the room door locked and never allow anyone inside without verifying the person and purpose.
13. Place a 'Do Not Disturb' sign on the door.
14. Check whether doors and windows are functioning properly and you are able to open the window.
15. Be suspicious of unusual calls. If they persist report to the management.
16. If you are staying for a long duration, change the room every week.
17. Prefer rooms in the middle and not far away from the lift. Never select a room which is nearer the fire escape.
18. As soon as you move into the room, get familiar with Fire Escape routes and memorise the same.
19. Be careful what you leave lying around in the room.
20. Never entertain strangers of either sex in the room. You may be trapped into Blackmail situations.
21. Hotel Fires are common occurrence. Be mentally prepared to meet one.
22. Never go out in the night alone. Keep to well lit respectable localities. Avoid danger zones- Prostitutes area, Hang outs for drug peddlers, waterfronts etc. Hotel staff can advice you what areas are to be avoided.
23. Never get involved in a quarrel, accident or a Bar room brawl. Withdraw from the scene and if necessary contact local police.
24. It will be a good idea to visit the Indian Embassy and get to know the Consuls. They can give you lot of advice on business and personal matters. Keep their telephone numbers handy.

# 7

# Managing a Crisis

INSPITE OF ALL precautions taken and preventive methods adopted, an Executive may be kidnapped and the miscreants may attack the organisation with extortious demands. To face these contingencies, every organisation should be prepared and ready. This calls for a Crisis Management Plan. We are not talking about anything new. In India, all major industries are required to have a Disaster Management Plan. These are prepared in consultation with the experts to deal with Man made and Natural disasters. These are read by one and all, rehearsed and updated periodically. We are suggesting that a similar plan be prepared to meet the threats from the miscreants.

The aim of any Crisis Management Plan should be:

1. To preserve lives;
2. To resolve the crisis with minimum loss of assets; and
3. To minimise dislocation to normal business/public operations.

Crisis Management is basically laying down organisational policy on responses, establishing operating procedures and setting up a committee to implement both. It aims at division of labour in times of crisis so that no single individual is exposed to enhanced responsibility and mental strain. A well formulated Crisis Management Plan builds up morale and confidence in any organisation.

To deal with crisis created by sky jackings, hostage taking, explosive threats etc. affecting the National Security, National

Governments have Cabinet Crisis Management Group consisting of the Head of the Government, Ministers of Defence, Interior, Civil Aviation and so on. This group has a permanent team of Senior Civil and Military officers known as Crisis Management Team. This team will have representatives of the Ministers mentioned above and in addition representatives of the Army and Specialist Counter Terrorist Forces. This team assembles as soon as any Crisis develops and acts on the basis of the decisions and policies decided by the Crisis Management Group of Ministers earlier. An elaborate administrative and logistical back up is provided to the team. It has world wide communication network and airlift capacity at its disposal. Nations have found that this system enables them to act quickly in an emergency cutting bureaucratic red tape and turf problems.

## Crisis Management Committee

First Step is to establish a Crisis Management Committee(CMC) at the Corporate Headquarters of the Organisation. It will be headed by the Chief Executive Officer of the organisation. He will be assisted by, and in his absence represented by, his deputy. There will be a full time Coordinator, who should be a very high ranking executive. Security, Finance, Legal, Personnel and Public Relations should be represented by the heads of the departments.

Second Step is to make a threat assessment. This task should be given to the Chief of Security and he, in consultation with the State Security and intelligence authorities, prepares and presents the same to the CMC. This assessment should be periodically and regularly updated.

Third Step is to establish systems for the free flow of and collection of information on a regular basis on the activities of the miscreants in the geographical area and its analysis to identify specific threats to the organisation. As this involves considerable expertise, it will be worthwhile to hire a specialist, who may brief the organisation from time to time on the updated threat scenario.

Fourth Step is to determine the policies of the organisation about specific responses. This will have to be taken to the Board Level and clearance obtained. This would include such things as whether ransom should be paid at all, if so, up to what limit, what steps are to be taken to evacuate the affected family, evacuation of the premises and personnel, Media Policy etc. Everyone in the CMC should be clear about these policy decisions.

Fifth Step is to establish liaison at the highest level with the various State and Security authorities. To be effective, not more than one department should be assigned to a member.

Sixth Step is to prepare a list of experienced consultants and negotiators for use in an emergency. All relevant details about them should be available to the CMC so that in an emergency it is possible to contact and hire them.

Seventh Step is to compile and have the updated Personal Profile Files of senior executives and their families, containing all personal details. (Please see the Format at the end)

The CMC should meet at periodical intervals and take up for discussion and serious consideration, hypothetical scenarios and the responses that could be offered. These exercises should be conducted in all seriousness and if possible a Consultant should act as the Observer and Devil's Advocate to pick holes in the proposed measures and responses. These exercises will make the CMC members constantly think of the possibility of something going wrong and mentally prepare them to deal with the problem in an emergency.

Where an organisation has extended operations spread across the country and overseas, depending on the threat perception in those areas, a smaller committee should be set up, which will act in cooperation and under the directions of the CMC. These committees could be designated as Local Crisis Management Teams (LCMT). The composition will have the same functional members representing the organisation at the local level.

## Response to A Crisis

When a crisis occurs, both the CMC and LCMT should go into session immediately and take stock of the situation. They should start implementing the previously decided upon steps, with such modifications as are necessary to suit the situation. For example, in the event of kidnapping of an executive, immediate measures will be initiated to protect the family and other vulnerable targets in the organisation. All will be alerted to watch out for communications from the kidnappers and the secretaries and telephone operators will be briefed, how to receive the messages from kidnappers and to communicate the same to the concerned without loss of time. Arrangements for recording the incoming messages will be made. A Negotiator and a Consultant will be appointed. Liaison with the local authorities will be established. If the event has taken place in a far off area, the CMC will keep constant touch with the LCMT and give it appropriate guidelines.

In other words, having gone through these steps in simulated hypothetical scenarios, the CMC will not find it difficult to take all these measures in its stride. There will be no panic, knee-jerk reaction or half hearted measures often complicating the situation.

Every organisation has its share of crisis. In the long run, it is advantageous to have a permanent CMC.

## Executive Personal Profile File

Name: Latest Photograph

Nickname/Pet Name:

Date of Birth:

Place of Birth:

Address:

Passport No.

Place and Date of Issue:

Driving License No.:

Place and Date of issue:

Particulars of Credit Cards:

Particulars of Membership of Clubs/
Professional Bodies:

Physical Measurements and Description:

Identifying Marks:

Blood Group:

Special Medical Requirements:

Names and Addresses of Family/
Personal Physician/ Dentist/ Pharmacist:

*Special Identifying Information*

Finger Prints (*Take Prints of Full Set of ten fingers*)

Writing Sample: (*One or two sentences in English and Local language to be written in ink.)*

Voice Recording in Tape: (*A short Message to be recorded in Normal voice*)

**(All these are to be kept in individual cellophane envelopes for comparison purposes in future)**

Particulars of close personal friends, with their contact Telephone Numbers and Addresses.

Particulars of Immediate Family, Wife and Children: Same details as for the Principal as outlined above.

Particulars of Relatives:(Full Personal Particulars as above except the Fingerprints, Hand writing Samples and Voice Recordings)

Father

Mother

Brothers

Sisters

***Note***: This data should be updated every year and kept in a Sealed Cover

# 8

# Hostage Negotiations

IN SPITE OF ALL the preventive and precautionary steps taken, the Executive may be actually kidnapped. What should be done? The Crisis Management Committee and the Local Management Team should be immediately called into session to work out the modalities of response.

All concerned should remember that the kidnapped Executive will be kept alive by the kidnappers till their demands are met. So, no harm will normally come to the victim unless some adventurist immature action is taken by those in charge of the matter. Further it should be kept in mind that in the past, over 90% of the kidnappings were for cash ransom. Only in 5%, there were demands for Publicity and in 3% there were Political demands. In a study of over 300 kidnappings world over, it was seen that in 90% of the cases, the victims survived the ordeal and no harm came to them. Only in 10% of the cases victims died due to natural causes, during police attempts to rescue them, and in a very few cases only, the kidnappers killed the victim, that too at the abduction stage when the victim put up a stout resistance or to prevent the victim from idenitifying them.

The priority should be to take care of the victim's family to prevent further secondary kidnappings to mount pressure on them and to save them from harassment by inquisitive people and the Media. It would be advisable to move them to a new location, and keep them incommunicado. However, the residence should be kept open and arrangements are to be made to attend to telephone calls. Kidnappers are bound to contact the family, or the victim's organisation or his close friends. It is necessary to advise everyone that telephone calls may come any time from the kidnappers and that the person responding should receive the call politely and elicit as much information as possible and immediately note down the message. The exact words used by the kidnappers are very important as they may give a clue to the identity of the group behind the kidnapping. Usually, the kidnappers will terminate the conversation in less than 50 seconds as they will be apprehensive that the telephone may be tapped and attempts will be made to trace the call.

Kidnappers would like to play on the psychological factor by using silence and time as their weapons. It is not unusual for the kidnappers to keep quite for a long period without contacting anyone just to raise the anxiety level. Means of communication of the kidnappers vary. In over 60% of the cases in the past, they have used the telephone to communicate their messages. In the rest, newspaper advertisements in code, messages to television networks, letters sent through Post or tapes containing the voice of the victim pleading for the payment of ransom played over the phone or sent through the Post or drops have been adopted.

The first intimation of the kidnapping may be a telephone call, a written or a taped message. In most of the cases it will be a terse and blunt telephone message informing the family that the executive is a hostage, and no harm will come to him if their instructions are followed. There will be a warning that the Police should not be contacted and if done, the hostage will be killed. The terms of ransom will be spelt out and the receiver of the call will be told to await further detailed instructions.

Since a lot would depend on the first call, as soon as it has been determined that the Executive has been kidnapped, all Secretaries and telephone operators in the office and the person attending the telephone call at the residence should be briefed about the way they should respond to the call and to take down the messages. A proforma should be prepared and be available near all telephones. If feasible, steps should be taken to record the incoming calls. A complete record of all calls received, time and duration and the exact verbatim record of the message etc. should be kept till the crisis is over.

After the first call, certain important decisions are to be taken. Police are to be informed at the very highest level possible so that they may take steps to keep the telephone under surveillance and to tape the future messages. A complete record or log of all events should be maintained chronologically. A decision has to be taken as to the quantum of ransom that could be offered in the negotiations. Family members will have to be consulted though they should be spared of actual participation in the operations. A negotiator should be carefully selected and a security consultant appointed to advise the negotiators on the steps to be taken.

## Qualities of A Negotiator

Hostage negotiations is a battle of wits and needs expertise. There is no place for amateurs and adventurers. Any failure will have fatal consequences. Normally, the negotiator should be a local person familiar with the geography, traditions and culture of the local people.

He should know the local language and the idiom. He should know how to negotiate. These criteria suggest that a lawyer or an executive dealing with industrial relations would be ideal. As far as possible, police officers should not be selected as negotiators unless they have undergone specialised courses in the art of Hostage negotiation. A close relative is unsuitable as he will not be able to negotiate with firmness. Top executive of the organisation should not be made a negotiator, for the reason that the negotiator will have to play for time by saying that he has to consult the boss to get approval. If the top policy maker is himself the negotiator, this opportunity will be lost. A negotiator should be willing to undertake the job. He must have the personal qualities to withstand the strain and the risks involved. He must be reliable, discreet and determined and have the nerve to withstand psychological pressures and threats. He must be capable of detached judgement.

Everyone cannot be a successful negotiator. In the first place, the negotiator has to establish his credibility with the kidnappers, project a neutral image, have a calming and soothing aura, have the capacity to focus on practical questions for solving the crisis and should be capable of avoiding political and philosophical arguments with the kidnappers. He should be cool under stress and keep the talks going at all costs and against all provocations. He should be capable of dealing fair and straight with the kidnapper and create a mutual trust and respect.

The kidnappers will be generally psychopaths either of paranoid, schizophronic, psychotic, depressive, anti-social and inadequate personalities. They are likely to take offence quickly and prone to violence. Any provocation will result in physical harm to the hostage. Thus the need for a negotiator with the qualities given above.

## Pre-Conditions

To be successful, hostage negotiations should have the following pre-conditions.

1. The authorities should have sufficient force or authority to take the life of the kidnapper, once arrested.
2. Good communications between the negotiator and the kidnapper should be established.
3. There should be an identified decision maker on either side.
4. The kidnapper should have a desire to live.
5. Availability of sufficient time to establish rapport between the kidnapper, the victim and the negotiator.
6. Credibility, power to make decisions and the authority of the negotiator should be established at the earliest point of time.
7. There should be restrictions on the movement of the kidnapper(s) i.e., police should be able to control their

8. There should be multiplicity of demands, many of them impossible, so that there is scope for bargaining.

## Stages of Negotiations

Negotiations often follow a predictable pattern. At the early stages the kidnapper dominates the proceedings. Once they find that the negotiator is firm and that their threats are not having any psychological impact on him, they climb down. At this stage, the negotiator dominates. In the final settlement phase, the negotiator will virtually dictate the terms. Like the game of chess, the hostage negotiations have three stages. The opening gambit - when the kidnapper pitches his demands and the negotiator gives an initial offer which is very low but attractive. Both sides then jockey for positions. When the negotiator senses the appropriate psychological moment, he clinches the deal. The end game is the delivery of ransom and the release of the hostage. For obvious reasons, we are not spelling out here various processes used. Any reputed security consultant would be able to advise about them with success. Depending on the Kidnapper's state of mind, there is need to get more specialists like Psycho-analysts to assist the negotiator.

At the appropriate stages of the negotiation, proof of life- that is, that the victim is alive should be demanded and verified. There have been cases when unrelated groups have negotiated and walked away with the ransom and cases where the kidnappers negotiated for ransom, after killing the victim. Delivery of ransom and release of the hostage are very delicate steps and any false move will result in fatalities. Just before delivery of the Ransom, proof that the hostage is alive should be demanded and only on satisfaction, ransom should be paid.

Release of hostage may not take place simultaneously with the payment of ransom. The miscreants need time to distribute the money and organise their escape plans. There is no alternative but to trust them and wait. Often, the hostages are released in different countries and jurisdictions to avoid police action.

It is easy to deal with the terrorists, organised crime and other well organised groups of miscreants. They are "Professionals" and have a stake to stay in the business. Normally they keep up their word and honour and their commitments. The real problem arises, when one is dealing with small time criminals, who have stumbled into the business of kidnapping. Often, the negotiator has to give them advice and professionalise them to ensure that no harm comes to the victim.

**Ethics**

It is often said that paying ransom is unethical and it encourages further kidnappings. While this is theoretically and morally a correct position, the purpose of ransom payment is to save a life and not to fill the coffers of the kidnappers. Except the victim, no one can take a position that no ransom will be paid and the victim can be allowed to die. Even National Governments, who have a clear cut policy of Non-negotiation, often allow the families to negotiate and pay the ransom. These are decided on case-to-case basis.

**Insurance**

In advanced countries, provision for taking out a ransom insurance policy is available. There are many restrictions and conditions and these policies are dealt with very confidentially. While these policies have proven to be useful to Mega Corporations, a debate is raging on the ethical aspects of the same.

It should be remembered that all man made crisis can be solved, if one displays patience, tact and wisdom. All failed hostage negotiations have been traced back to human failures due to want of one of the these three qualities.

# 9

# Know Your Enemy

We have been using the Term Miscreants to describe a wide spectrum of elements like Terrorists, Extremists, Organised Crime and others. It is necessary for the Executive to know little more in detail about them.

## Political Violent Elements

These are groups of individuals, who wish to change the existing political system in the country and often of the World through violence. They have no patience for democratic and peaceful means. Since the majority of the population do not share their enthusiasm for violence, they wish to use violence to convert them to their view and to force them into submission out of fear. Out of these elements, for the purpose of our discussion, terrorists are the most relevant.

There are national and international groups.

TERRORISTS, are those, who being in a minority, try to use the fear of death to force the majority to accept their demands and political philosophy. There are National, International and Special Interest Groups of Terrorists.

## National Terrorist Groups

In India, we have the Khalistanis or the Sikh Militants, Jammu and Kashmir Liberation Front, United Liberation Front of

Assam, Naga underground movements and so on. We have also Political Extremists like the Peoples War Group of Andhra Pradesh, Religious Groups like Anand Marg, and others. All these movements need money to propagate their message. In the past, they used to rob Banks and Government Treasuries to replenish their coffers. Now, they find it easy to kidnap the Business Executives and extract huge ransoms. Since these people do not have any value for human life, the responses to their threat should be calculated and deliberated.

Almost all these groups get guidance, training, Arms and ordnance from unfriendly powers. Of late, the Veneer of political ideology has been rubbed off and most of these groups have virtually become Criminal Gangs.

Recall the incidents of kidnapping of Mr.Doraiswamy by the JKLF; Mr. Baruah by the ULFA and Mr. Rado the Rumanian Diplomat by the Khalistanis.

## International Terrorist Groups

Well known Terrorist Groups like Irish National Army, Red Army Brigade of Italy and Japan, Badder-Meinhof group of the Red Army Faction of Germany, Palestinian Liberation Organisation and various other Palestinian Groups, Islamic Groups like Hezbollah, LTTE and others, undertake terrorist action in concert with National groups. In their case, it is mostly for Publicity and rarely for money. They normally attack well known Multi Nationals and their Executives.

## Special Interest Group Terrorists

Of late, well meaning respectable people belonging to Special Interest Groups like Anti Nuclear War Groups; Animal Welfare Groups; Environmental Groups; Anti-abortion Groups, etc. have started using terrorist tactics and violence to further their cause. Often they attack the Executives of the Multinationals and other organisations engaged in research, development and other constructive work, which in their view is opposed to their cause.

## Extreme Fringe Religious and Cult Groups

Not a single day passes without Newspapers reporting the activities of weird extreme fringe religious, ethnic, Neo-Nazi, Fascist and other groups staging spectacular yet bizarre incidents. Since these people do not care for either their own or others lives, often they indulge in almost suicidal attacks on Business Executives. Mostly their aim is publicity.

## Organised Crime

In almost all developed and developing countries, Crime is being organised like big business. The well known example is Mafia of Italy and the USA. These organisations thrive on Gun running, Drug peddling, white slave traffic, prostitution loan sharking and protection rackets. They are very powerful and almost run a parallel government. Their writ run everywhere. Often they indulge in kidnapping of business executives for ransom and they usually go for very big fish.

They also undertake contract killing and Product contamination and market destruction for a price from the business rivals. In our Country Metropolitan Cities of Bombay and Delhi have already come under the shadow of organised crime. Other cities are fast catching up. In USA, they try to control retail outlets and franchise stations and through use of violence, extract large sums of money as protection fees to carry on legitimate business. They do not look for any apology for their activities and never cite political ideology to justify their actions. They are ruthless. They can be fought only by the Police.

## Ordinary Criminals

Lured by the success of major kidnapping cases brought about by professional groups, ordinary criminals often indulge in kidnapping of Business Executives and extract ransom. They also indulge in extortion rackets. The most dangerous aspect of these cases is that these criminals are not professionals, it is very difficult to judge their intentionsand reactions. Often, they act in panic and ruthlessly. One has to deal with them literally with kid gloves and often teach them the nuances. At the least provocation they would kill or maim or violate the person of the hostage. They are easy to be trapped but we must always keep in mind the safety of the kidnapped victim.

It will be seen that the prime motivation to cause harm to the Business Executive by these miscreants is to extract money through ransom. If the preventive measures suggested are taken, it will be possible to throw them off the scent.

# 10

# Means of Destruction of the Miscreants

INTERNATIONAL, NATIONAL and Intra-national Terrorists, Organised Crime and Common Criminals have access to and acquire sophisticated means of destruction and use them to their great advantage. One of the unintended spin-offs of the collapse of the Communist Block is the easy availability of lethal means of destruction at the market place. While it is the responsibility of the National Governments to disposses the miscreants of these means of destruction, as potential victims, Business Executives should at least be aware of these. There are rapid advances in Science and Technology in the sphere of destruction. What has been listed here is not exhaustive; newer and more lethal means of destruction are being added everyday to this never ending list. The purpose of enumeration is not to create fear and panic but to create an awareness. Forewarned is Forearmed. To complete the picture, we have also given details of Detection and Preventive equipment, which could be used with advantage in neutralising these threats.

While on an 'operation', the miscreants take into consideration, the following factors:

(a) ***Easy availability*** : It should be possible to procure the equipment without much difficulty at the site of use;

(b) ***Popular caliber*** : In the case of weapons, the miscreants will opt for popular caliber to ensure continuity in the supply of ammunition;

(c) ***Portability or ease of concealment*** : To attain the maximum impact, the miscreant would like to have the element of surprise on his side. Concealment and portability help in these.

(d) ***Reliability and assurance of quality of performance*** : Since the miscreants plan their moves very carefully and actions are based on split second coordination, they cannot afford to have equipment, whose reliability and quality of performance is ever in doubt.

(e) ***Simplicity of operations*** : Since the tasks of destruction may be allotted to anyone in the group, it should be possible for everyone to handle the equipment. They cannot search for specialists in an emergency; finally,

(f) ***Assured destruction potential*** : Since the aim of the miscreants is to spread fear and terror among the target audience, the equipment deployed should have the maximum destruction potential.

## Firearms

Pistols, both machine and normal varieties, revolvers, all kinds of portable automatic weapons are used to harm the potential victims. Different types of ammunition, silencers, telescopes and various other attachments are used, based on the actual needs.

Once the miscreant reaches the target within the shooting range, it is very difficult to avoid casualties. Metal Detectors and X-Ray equipment, if used judiciously, will reveal concealed weapons. Bullet Proof Vests/Jackets, B.B.Briefcases etc. can give protection at short range.

## Projectiles

Generally used to destroy physical objects like buildings, trains, aircrafts etc. and are rarely used to eliminate persons. These are Mortars, Missiles, Rockets etc. Only means of protection against these are the physical barriers. Though anti-missile technology can be used with success, the cost is prohibitive. Projectiles need distances. It is therefore necessary that the threatened Facility should have an effective patrolling of the area far beyond the perimeter to detect unfriendly activities.

## Explosives (*Bombs*)

Explosives are of two kinds viz. Explosive Ordnance Devices (EODs) and Improvised Explosive Devices (IEDs).

*EOD*s - Mines, Grenades, Gelatine Sticks etc. come under this category. They are available for use in the Defence Forces or with Industrial users. They come in ready to use form. Mostly they are stolen from legitimate users or bought in the black market.

*IED*s - They are fabricated by the Miscreants to create the maximum damage to unsuspecting victims. They come in many shapes and sizes. Usually, they are concealed in articles of daily use. Main components of the IEDs are: Power Source, Switch, Detonator and the Explosives.

Power source could be electrical or non-electrical. Electrical switches could be Remote control, Timing Devices, Pressure based, Pull, Release, Electronic etc. Non-electrical switches could be Pull, Release, Mechanical, Time Pencil, Chemical Timers etc. Detonators could be Plain and normal varieties or Electrical.

Explosives used could be Low Explosives like Black Powder, Smokeless Powder etc. High Explosives are RDX, PETN, TETRYL, TNT, NG etc.

### Detection Equipment

Metal Detectors, Wire/Cable Detector, Electronic Stethoscope, Fibrescope, X-Ray, Vapour and Particles Detection Systems etc. Humans through visual search and the Sniffer Dogs have a great role to play in the detection of explosives. It has been estimated that Humans can detect upto 35% of the explosives through visual search; equipment can detect upto 50%; dogs upto 90%. Therefore, experts advise use of all the three to ensure near total detection.

**Prevention Equipment**

Electronic Frequency Jammers; Bomb Blankets, Bomb Suits etc.

The emphasis should be on detection of the bomb or the IED, and to cordon it off. Neutralisation is a highly technical skill and will have to be attempted only by the experts.

## Chemical Agents

**Natural**

Lead, Arsenic, Mercury, Herbs, Micro Organisms etc. Can be detected with the use of Toxic Material Detection Kit. There are many sophisticated equipment available in the market. Protective Gas Mask and Gas Suits will help.

## Man Made Toxic Chemical Agents

| | | |
|---|---|---|
| Nerve Gases | : | Sarin; Soman; Tabun;VX etc. |
| Suffocating Agents | : | Phosgene, Chlorine, etc. |
| Blood Toxins | : | Cyanogen, Cyanide, Chloride formulations etc. |
| Pesticides | : | Endrin, Parathion, Diazinon, Malathion, etc. |
| Irritants | : | Arsine, Chloroacetophenone, Chloropierene, etc. |
| Incapacitants | : | LSD, Mescaline, etc. |

KGB had used in the past with great success, the Poison Dart to kill their opponents silently in public places.

Toxic Material Detection Kit can help in detection. Gas Masks and Gas suits will help in protection.

## Biological Agents

Living organisms like Virus, Bacteria, Anthrax etc. and Inorganic Toxins have been used.

## Radioactive Elements

There are many Radioactive elements which can be used successfully to eliminate large number of people. It has been estimated that some International Terrorist Groups have the potentiality to make Nuclear Devices. They have so far not been used. There are sophisticated equipment to detect radio activity which is created in the atmosphere when these elements are moved about. There are special procedures for decontaminating an area and also to treat the effects of Radiation

## Materials used for Arson

Thermite etc. are used with oxidants and Napalm, White Phosphorous, Sodium etc. are used without oxidants. Presence of these materials can be detected with the help of special equipment.

While planning defence against these threats, it should be kept in mind that prevention is always better than cure. We should concentrate more on preventive steps after making a rational threat assessment. Government agencies have enormous resources at their disposal, particularly in dealing with the threats from the explosives. Closest cooperation and coordination with the authorities will be in our interest.

# 11

# Dealing with Threats from Explosives

EXPLOSIVES ARE commonly used by the miscreants to destroy property, for blackmail and extortion, and sometimes for killing people. Except in the cases of "Human Bomb", where the person who sets off the explosion himself is killed, in all other cases explosives are set to explode after some lapse of time, to enable the planters to leave the scene unharmed. With modern advances in timing devices, explosives can be primed to explode after a delay of few days and even weeks. Electronic triggering systems make it easy for the miscreant to explode the bomb at his will. With the advent of plastic explosives, it is possible to make a bomb in any shape of commonly used household or office item. They can also be concealed in items of daily use.

It is known that often miscreants do alert the intended victim, about the planting of the explosives on the premises and warn them about the time of explosion. This advance warning will generally come before a few minutes, probably giving sufficient time for the place to be evacuated. The miscreant will never give the location of the bomb. All threats should be taken as real, unless the contrary is proved. It is true, often hoax calls are received from the pranksters, mentally deranged persons etc. This is no justification to ignore a warning.

Whether at home or office, every one should be trained how to react to the call, how to summon help and how to ensure orderly evacuation. A scheme of action or a drill should be formulated and rehearsed often to enable familiarity with the steps involved.

## Instructions for the Person Receiving the Information

(*a*) **If by Mail** : Preserve the envelop and the letter carefully in a cellophane cover and hand over the same to the Chief Security Officer or to the Seniormost Executive to take further action. Do not discuss the contents of the threat with anyone, till you have been questioned by the authorities or by the Police. The purpose of this injunction is to ensure that the facts are clear in your mind and your memory has not been superimposed by the views expressed by others in the matter. When your memory is fresh, note down how the letter reached you, mode of delivery, the date, time and circumstances etc. If the writing on the envelope or the letter resembles the handwriting of someone known to you, note down this fact also. This will help you in furnishing answers to the questions that may be asked of you by the authorities.

(*b*) **If over the telephone**: Every Secretary or Telephone operator in the office should have the following proforma ready with her and endeavour to fill as many items as possible.

## Explosive Threat Reporting form Important Notice

We need your help to meet the threat from explosive and save the lives and property of this organisation. So please be calm; courteous to the caller; listen to the caller patiently without interruption. If you display courtesy and empathy, the caller may give out many details like the purpose behind the Mission and where the bomb is secreted, so on. As you are talking to the caller, use the prearranged signal to notify your Superiors, Security Officer, Colleagues, so that they may also listen in and if possible they may notify the police or the Telephone authorities to trace the call. Never threaten or frighten the caller. Remember that the caller has all the information and if he hangs up, there is no way, we can get any information about the explosives.

## Proforma

Date/ Time of the call:
Exact words used by the caller:
Get from the caller replies to these points in a tactful manner

1. When is the Bomb going to explode?
2. Where is the Bomb right now?
3. What kind of Bomb is it?
4. What does it look like?
5. Why was it placed?

## From Your Impression of the Caller, Circle the Appropriate Factors

| | | |
|---|---|---|
| 1. | **Identity of the Voice** | : Male/Female/Adult/ Juvenile/Child/Elderly Person. |
| 2. | **Characteristics of the Voice** | : Loud/Soft/High Pitched/ Deep/Raspy/Pleasant/ Drunken/others |
| 3. | **Accent** | : Local/Regional/Foreign. *(Note down whose voice in the circle of your friends and associates it resembles)* |
| 4. | **Mode of Speech** | : Fast/Slow/Distinct/ Distorted/Nasal/Slurred/ Lisping/Stammering/ Stuttering. |
| 5. | **Language used** | : Abusive/Foul/Good/Fair/ Respectable/Cultured. |
| 6. | **Manner of Caller** | : Angry/Calm/Rational/ Irrationaol/Incoherent/ Coherent |

7. **Background Noises** : Machines/Factory/ Trains/ Trams/Motor Vehicles/ Market Place/ Street Traffic /Air conditioner / Aeroplane/ Bedlam/others (Specify).

8. Any other information you can recollect.

Signature
Designation

## Immediate Action

Please hand over this form to your Security Officer at once. Do not discuss about the call with anyone till you are interviewed by the police or your security. Discussions with others will make your memory blurred.

## Action by the Person Receiving the above Report

1. Notify the local Police, Fire and Medical Services immediately.
2. Seek the assistance of the Bomb Disposal Squad and the Sniffer Dogs.
3. Inform the Senior Management of the threat.
4. If the caller has specified the area, immediately evacuate the area of all non-essential personnel and cordon it off. Commence search with the help of security and safety department personnel.
5. If the threat is of general nature, request top management to issue instructions to all managers to commence search for any unidentified object in their areas. Security and safety personnel should concentrate their searches on the most vulnerable areas.
6. Do not allow any visitors to enter the premises till the searches are over.

7. Media should be kept at bay and should be handled by the Police only.

## Action when an Unidentified Object is Found

1. Evacuate that area.
2. Keep sand bags around the object. Never on top of the object.
3. Keep all the doors and windows open.
4. Reduce opportunities for Fire, by removing all combustible material from the vicinity of the object.
5. Await the arrival of Police / Bomb Disposal Squad.
6. Do not handle the object or pour water on that or immerse it in water.
7. Communicate brief physical description of the object to Police/Bomb Disposal Squad.
8. Communicate the details, physical description to all other departments / sections, so that in their search, they may look for a similar device.
9. Only after the object has been taken possession by the Police/B.D.Squad and they clear the area for people to enter the premises, allow personnel to re-enter the premises.
10. No one knows the exact power of the explosive device. It is therefore advisable that all personnel, except those needed for operations, be kept away at a very safe distance.

## Preparing the Employees for Bomb Threats

If you are in a locality known for violent activities by the miscreants, you should prepare the personnel to face the Bomb Threat. This is best done by:

(a) Holding special briefing sessions for the Secretaries/ Telephone operators about the procedure to be followed by them when they receive a Threat Call. They should practice on filling the Bomb Threat Reporting Form.

(*b*) Brief all personnel, preferably by the Security Department, about the Drill to be followed. Prepare a concise Circular about the DOs and DONTs and circulate it to all personnel.
(*c*) Rehearse evacuation procedures.
(*d*) At least once in Six months, have a Mock Exercise.

## At Home

Brief your family members and the domestic help not to accept Parcels, Bouquets, etc. from strangers and bring them into the living area. They should also report finding any new or strange object in the House or in the Grounds. Keep the Garage locked at all the time. No strangers, salesmen and vendors should be allowed inside the house and they should never be left alone. Any object left behind by them should be treated with suspicion.

## Dealing with Letter Bomb

Explosives in the garb of Letters or Parcels have created havoc in the past. They have been used by all types of miscreants. These are difficult to detect and normally fit into a Business envelop. They can kill and cause very serious injuries even to the persons at some distance. Letter bombs have become very lethal with the introduction of the powerful plastic explosive - C-4.

C-4 is generally manufactured in sheets, of a foot wide and half an inch thick. It can be cut, moulded, rolled and shaped into any form. It is neutral in colour and does not emit any pungent odour. It can be exploded with the help of a miniature electronic primer of the size of Ball pen refill. The explosive is made to look like an ordinary letter and the triggering mechanism is embedded in the middle. The striker is primed with the help of a lever and a hair thin wire holds the same in the place and is pasted at the mouth of the envelop. When the unsuspecting victim opens the letter by tearing off the edges, the hair thin wire is released, which in turn lets go the lever and the triggering mechanism instantly gets activated and the C-4 explodes.

As the Mail are opened in the Mail Room or by the Secretaries, even though the letters are addressed to high Executives, it is these personnel who get killed or injured. At home, the domestics or the children open the envelope and get killed or maimed. It is possible to prevent these mishaps. An inexpensive Letter Bomb detector is available in the market. When the Mail is passed through them, if there is a wire or a triggering mechanism, the equipment gives a warning. It is necessary to brief all the secretaries and Mail Room personnel about the precautions to be taken. Similarly, at home also, all should be briefed.

Parcels, Gifts, Bulky Books, Bouquets etc. received from unknown persons should be treated with suspicion and should be examined for tell-tale signs of ticking clock works, protruding wires, pungent smells etc. All suspicious objects should be treated with caution and care. Portable X-Ray systems are available in the market and these are to be installed in big organisations. While it may not be possible to eliminate all risks from explosives, they can be reduced by creating awareness and taking the precautions outlined above.

# 12

# Case Studies of Kidnapping of Executives

STUDY OF SPECIFIC instances of kidnapping of Executives that have taken place in the past, would enable the readers to understand the circumstances that made such kidnapping possible, the methods adopted by the miscreants and the responses to the incidents by the organisations, police and the families. We have selected the following well known cases for a descriptive study as each one of them conveys very valuable lessons to the Executives. The Adage 'Wise men learn from others experience and not so wise(Fools) from their own' can apply to the threats from kidnappings. While going through these, the Executive should actively consider, how such an incident could have been avoided and if he were the victim, how he would have responded to the event.

Latin America is the cradle of Political Violent Movements. Till, 1971, Latin American Terrorists were attacking Government Treasuries, Banks etc. to fund their movements. When one of the groups succeeded in kidnapping a Business Executive and forced a Multinational firm to do their bidding, the idea of Kidnapping the Executives to fill their coffers took deep routes in their minds. According to an estimate, over a five year period alone, People's Revolutionary Party (PRP) and MONTONEROS ( Armed wing of the Trotskyite Revolutionary Workers Party, netted US$ 30 million and US$ 240 millions respectively.

There was a spate of kidnappings in the decade following 1971. This was helped by the fact that over 400 US Firms had their branches in Latin America and many US Nationals were working in them in senior positions. The Communist rhetoric against capitalist Yankees, found a sympathetic response among the poor and the downtrodden. In the process of filling their coffers with the ransom extracted from US Firms, the terrorists also became the good Samaritans and Robinhoods, by ensuring that the poor also got a bit of the cake.

We discuss the following cases in detail, as each one of them has an important message to convey to business executives.

Kidnapping of Born Brothers
Kidnapping of Niehouse
Kidnapping of Leon Don Richardson
Kidnapping of Heineken
Kidnapping of Baron Empain

## Kidnapping of Born Brothers

Highest ransom for a kidnapping, U.S.$ 60 million was paid in this case. This is an instance to prove the need for expertise to deal with the kidnappers. Had a professional consultant or a negotiator been employed in this case, the ransom would have been much smaller.

### Facts

BUNGE BORN, largest business conglomerate in Latin America, was known to be very prosperous and the owners very rich. The Founder-President, Mr. Bunge was getting old and his two sons were slated to take over the management of the firm. Every morning, both the sons used to drive together to office from their home for 24 Kms outside Buenos Aires. Their general manager used to sit in the front seat along with the driver. Their car was followed by an escort car with two armed bodyguards. On most occasions, a third car carrying the children of Born family used to follow the escort car and it used to drop off near the school. This routine made it necessary for the brothers to start at the same time everyday and take the same route to their office.

## The Kidnap

On the morning of September 16, 1974, the Monteneros staged the kidnap. Using 19 terrorists, they chose a broad road and simulated road maintenance work and diverted the traffic. They blocked all narrow service roads on the sides. Two trucks were used to ram into the Cars of the Born Brothers and the escort. Terrorists dressed as police, 'arrested' the bodyguards and handcuffed them to their own vehicle. They shot the general manager and the driver and whisked away the Born brothers. As violent incidents were common place at that time, none of the bystanders took any notice of the event.

## Response

A week later, the kidnappers established contacts with the Father through secret telephone messages and written communications. On October 2, they demanded US$100 million as ransom. They also demanded that the Firm should change their labour policies and distribute goods to the poor. Bunge Born initially offered 17.5 million and later raised it to 30 million. The kidnappers insisted that the starting price for the negotiations will be 50 million. When Bunge Born expressed his inability to raise the sum, they offered to release one of the brothers for half the sum and the other, after the balance has been paid. Later, they hardened their stand.

Meanwhile, Jorge Baron, one of the kidnapped brothers himself negotiated with the kidnappers and agreed for the payment of the ransom of US$60 million and sent written instructions for the Firm to pay up. This was accordingly done. The money was paid both in Argentina and in Switzerland. The younger brother Juan was released on March 22, 1975 after the payment of ransom, but the kidnappers refused to release the elder brother. As demanded by the terrorists, Food, Blankets and Clothing were to be distributed to poor in 150 places and striking workers were paid for the duration they were on strike. On June 20, 1975, Jorge was released.

## Kidnapping of William Niehous

This case is interesting from these points:

1. The victim was held captive for a record duration of 1219 days.
2. There was no demand for ransom but for some public charity.
3. Compliance with the demands of kidnappers, brought the Firm in conflict with local authorities.
4. The victim was released by the Police by chance in one of the routine confrontation with the Terrorists.
5. The determination and self confidence of the victim while in custody.

## Background

William Niehous, was the vice president of the US Giant Owen-Illinois subsidiary in Venezuela. He was living in the suburbs of the capital, Caraças. The 'Commando Argimiro Gabaldon' a splinter group of the 'Bandar Roja', Terrorist movement executed the kidnapping.

## The Kidnap

On the night of Friday, February 27, 1976, seven masked men armed with automatic weapons burst into the residence of Niehous, tied up his wife, an American maid, three teenage sons and kidnapped Niehous. They whisked him into the jungles. On Monday, a local newspaper printed the Manifesto from the kidnappers that Niehous has been 'arrested and imprisoned' and is being tried at a 'People's court' for interfering with the internal affairs of Venezuela. The group mentioned that they were not interested in the ransom and if Police took any action to trace the victim, he would be killed. Police traced the vehicle in which the victim was transported by the kidnappers and some personal clothing of Niehous. Mrs. Niehous recognised that three of the abductors, had earlier worked in their house as grass cutters and police established that two of them were prison escapees and Terrorists.

The kidnappers communicated to the authorities three demands:

1. That their Political Manifesto should be published in Newspapers in Venezuela, New York, London and Paris.
2. That the Firm Owen-Illinois distribute 1200 food baskets in Venezuela.
3. That the Firm pay each of its 1600 Venezuelan employees a bonus of approximately US$116 each.

## Response

For six weeks there were no developments and the efforts of the Police to trace Niehous proved fruitless. The group sent a photograph of the victim in the company of a masked armed Terrorist. The threat to the life of the victim was to be taken seriously. The Firm caved in to the demands and published the Manifesto in New York, Paris and London and also paid the bonus to the employees. This publication infuriated the local Government and they promptly nationalised the Firm. Inspite of the conditions having been met, the kidnappers did not release the victim.

Niehous was made to trudge through the jungle in the company of kidnappers. He was treated well, though was always chained to a tree or a pole. He did not attempt to escape and maintained good rapport with his captors. He kept himself physically and mentally fit. He was determined to live and get reunited with his family.

One day in a routine patrolling and combing operation by the Security Forces, Niehous was noticed and was rescued. This was mere accident.'

William Niehous described his ordeal in great detail and gave valuable advice to business executives, in Marti Herz(ed)- *DIPLOMAT AND TERRORISTS ; WHAT WORKS AND WHAT*

*DOESN'T* (Georgetown University, Washington 1982) and Brian Jenkins(ed) -*TERRORISM AND PERSONAL PROTECTION* (Butterworths, Boston, 1985). These two books are to be read by all executives. We summarise below, the suggestions made by Niehous in these works.

## Suggestions of Niehous for Surviving Captivity

1. Try to make your captors recognise you as a human being. Be humane.
2. Communicate with the captors.
3. Set individual goals-however hopeless the situation may appear.
4. Eat and exercise.
5. Have faith in God and Humanity, Family and Friends.
6. Take seriously the threat of kidnapping and adopt preventive measures.
7. Be unpredictable - Very routine.
8. Share all financial information with the family, as a matter of routine.

According to Niehous, a noted psychologist converted his suggestions into a simple easy to remember acronym - **'F A C E S'**, which stands for:

**F** **FAITH**
**A** **ASPIRATIONS OR GOALS**
**C** **COMMUNICATION**
**E** **EATING**
**S** **SENSITIVITY, BEING HUMAN**

## Kidnapping of Leon Don Richardson

This case vividly brings out the following:

1. The courage and determination of the victim.
2. The crucial role played by the consultant.
3. The valuable assistance of Negotiator.
4. What a well trained and briefed staff can do in an emergency.

## Background

Leon D.Richardson, was the Founder President of Magna Industrial Co.Ltd, a multi national metal group based in Australia and Hongkong. It had operations worldwide. His partner and son-in-law, Dundon was also based in Australia and there was perfect understanding between the two. They had a very competent Office Manager Gloria Donaldson. As part of his business travels, Richardson visited Guatemala.

## The Kidnap

On February 10, 1981, Richardson, who was in Guatemala only for two days, started early with two of his local officers on a round of meeting his clients and prospective customers. They were all travelling together in the car of one of the local employees. They completed visits to two factories and were in the third one. As they emerged from this factory and were walking towards the car, they were surrounded by eight terrorists, five men and three women armed with automatic weapons. They moved very quickly and pushed the local employees spread-eagled on their car. Richardson was physically lifted and was hurled into a pick up van. His hands and feet were tied and some abductors sat on his back to keep him down. He was blindfolded and taken out of the city. He was imprisoned in a dark underground cell for hundred days in a rural area.

The Chief of the kidnappers questioned him at great length from a list of written questions and Richardson thought they were double checking whether he was speaking the truth. He was asked to nominate a negotiator and Richardson named his son-in-law and partner in business. He was warned not to do anything silly and to cooperate. Richardson knew at that point of time, that he will not be killed and he immediately mentioned about his heart ailment and gave a list of medicines he needed. These were supplied to him regularly.

Richardson decided to fight it out with his captors psychologically. He alternated the behaviour of being cooperative and aggressive. He demanded and got the type of food he wanted, books to read and stationery to write. He kept a psychological distance from the kidnappers so that he may not fall a victim to Stockholm syndrome. He tried to bribe a guard to escape and actually attempted escape twice. He exercised regularly and kept himself fit.

## The Response

After Richardson named Dundon as a negotiator, it was decided that the negotiations will take place in Mexico. As soon as the news of kidnapping reached him, Dundon got in touch with a firm of reputed security consultants and acted on their advice all through. While playing down the importance of Richardson to the company affairs in media, Dundon highlighted the medical condition of Richardson and the need for him to take his daily medicines. On February 16, Dundon visited Mexico and established contact with the consultant and his local staff. The consultant briefed him about the tactics of kidnappers and how he could resist their domination over him psychologically.

The first contact from the kidnappers came on March 20, in Richardson's Sydney office. This call was taken by Gloria Donaldson. The caller asked that Dundon should be in a designated Hotel on March 22nd. There was a telex also purported to be from Richardson and from the wordings, Dundon knew it was a bogus one. Since he was not sure whether he was dealing with the real kidnappers, he sent two of his representatives to visit Mexico. They were contacted by a female kidnapper and were told that business would be transacted with Dundon only. Two days later, Gloria again received a call from the kidnappers, who insisted that they would speak to Dundon only. Gloria gave a proof of life question to be answered by Richardson.

On April 14, the kidnappers again contacted Gloria and gave the right answer to the proof of life question. The kidnappers also gave some personal information about Gloria's family to confirm that they are in fact in touch with

Richardson. The kidnappers again contacted Gloria on the 15th and insisted that Dundon should meet them in Mexico. It was settled that Dundon would make his own arrangements for stay and he could be contacted in three days time in Mexico. Further proof of life question was given to them to reply when they contacted Dundon. They insisted that Dundon should play fair and this was agreed to. Dundon took the advice of the security consultant and handled the kidnappers very firmly and met them on his own terms. The kidnappers delivered a hand written letter from Richardson and a tape of his own voice. Dundon could make out that the recording was made under duress. A secret telephone number was fixed and a contact was named. Prolonged negotiations were held and the demands were scaled down and finally an undisclosed sum was agreed upon. In the meantime, unaware of these developments, Richardson put on a rage act and gave an ultimatum to the kidnappers, that if he was not released in two days time, he would commit suicide. Coincidentally, Richardson was released within that period in Guatemala city on May 20th, in front of Red Cross Building. He was safe and sound, but had lost 35 Kgs in weight.

There is a controversy whether the ransom was actually paid or not. Some people believe that as Richardson threatened to commit suicide and as the collaborators of kidnappers were arrested by Mexican Police, Richardson was released. Dundon on oath of confidentiality never confirmed or denied the payment of ransom, which was reported to be US$1 million.

Full story of Richardson's case appears in Kevin Sinclair: ***Kidnap: A Victims Story*** -Ted Thomas Ltd., Hongkong-1982 and in Richardson's own words in Brian Jenkins-***TERRORISM AND PERSONNEL PROTECTION*** (op. cit.), pp. 407-422.

Richardson's Rules for Survival in a Kidnapping

1. Avoid going to high risk countries, unless you have a dire need to do so.
2. Take sensible security precautions.
3. Assess the risks.
4. Study kidnapping cases.
5. Get ready to react positively.

6. Mentally prepare yourself for a kidnapping.
7. Take expert advice. "Anti-kidnap advisors are worth their weight in gold".
8. Prepare to survive under any cost.
9. Keep your dignity. Keep an upper hand over the kidnappers.
10. Pay the ransom. If possible, take out ransom insurance. "Human life is more important than money".
11. Bring in Police at the earliest point of time.

Richardson was a brave man and had extraordinary strength of will power and courage. Very few can emulate his example. Yet, this study will show an instance of great courage under adverse situations.

## Kidnapping of Frederick Heineken

This case is interesting from the point that even though the victim had advance warning that he is likely to be a victim of kidnapping, he relied on Security Hardware and failed to take simple personal security measures like varying the routine. Personal security calls for proper attitude and sophisticated equipment can not replace the need for personal involvement. When specific risks are known, a round the clock vigilance is indicated. Miscreants look for weak links in the arrangements and exploit them.

### Facts

Freddie Heineken was the Chairman of the Beer company which bore his name. He possessed great wealth, maintained a very high profile and was recognised throughout his country as an influential man in west European politics. He was close to the Dutch Royal Family. He was an ideal target for kidnapping. His friend, Caranas was kidnapped in October 1977 in Amsterdam and was released after payment of ransom. During the investigation of Caranas case. Police recovered a diary which clearly indicated that the miscreants were planning to kidnap Heineken. He was duly advised of the threat. He immediately took number of precautions to protect himself, buying extensive security equipment, erected fences around his house, introduced a system of guards and dogs, and bought an armoured car for personal use. Apparently, all these were being studied by the kidnappers, who located a chink in the arrangements and successfully carried out the kidnapping.

## The Kidnap

On November 9, 1983 at 7 p.m., as Heineken left his office and was moving towards his waiting car, he was overtaken by two masked men, who forced him to walk towards a Mini-van standing nearby. Heineken called to his driver, who rushed to his help. Both were mercilessly beaten and thrown into the van. A third kidnapper was driving the Mini-van. The van was found shortly after with the engine running. Investigations revealed that the van was stolen, four months earlier. Three hours after the kidnapping, a packet was found outside the The Hague Police Station containing Heineken's watch and the driver's passport and a note that US$13 million equivalent ransom should be paid and with instructions for the wording of an advertisement to indicate compliance.

## The Response

The Heineken company dealt with this matter as a family affair and decided to pay the ransom. They also cooperated with Dutch Police, who undertook to keep a low profile and not to interfere with the negotiations. The company placed the advertisements on November 11 and 12, requesting for contact. On November 16, they received instructions to start the payment of ransom, which was ignored, instead, the company placed an advertisement refusing payment without further contact and repeated it for two days. The kidnappers established contact and by November 23, the terms were finalised. The kidnappers agreed to provide Proof of Life before the payment of the ransom and would also release the victims immediately.

As per the instructions of the kidnappers, the ransom money was placed in postal mail bags and was carried in a white van with Red Cross markings. A single driver started out on November 28 on a journey of over 150 miles guided by the kidnappers before, he received instructions to stop the van on a viaduct and throw the money sacks down to a waiting truck. Inspite of the payment of the ransom, the victims were not released.

Simultaneously, police were keeping all notorious criminals under watch. Concerned with the safety of the victims, police launched simultaneous raids on many hideouts. In one, by luck and happy coincidence, they found both the victims in their undergarments, chained to concrete pillars. They were released. Subsequently the police arrested large number of criminals and recovered most of the ransom.

Investigations revealed that the kidnapping was carried out by a three member professional gang of criminals, led by the son of a former Heineken employee.

## Kidnapping of Baron Empain

This case illustrates the value of time gained through negotiations and the excellent cooperation between the victim's family and the police.

### Facts

Baron Empain, a 41 year old Belgian millionaire was well known throughout Europe for his wealth and riches. As a spate of kidnappings was sweeping Europe at that time, Baron instructed his wife that in the event of his kidnapping, the family should not pay any ransom.

### The Kidnap

On January 24, 1978, as Baron was emerging from his house

on his way to work from his French Residence, three armed men kidnapped him. This was the handiwork of criminals, though many Terrorist groups tried to claim credit to hog publicity. Police launched massive searches and road blocks with no success. Meanwhile, the kidnappers established contact with the family and demanded equivalent of U.S.$ 25 million.

## The Response

The family refused to respond. After three days, the criminals chopped off one of fingers of the Baron and mailed it to the family. Fearing for the safety of the Baron, the family started negotiations and the police were fully in the picture. A ransom of US$8 million was agreed after two months of negotiations. The ransom was delivered under police surveillance and one of the officers hiding in the boot of the car shot one of the miscreants collecting the ransom and another was arrested. As there is death penalty for kidnapping resulting in the death of the victim, this criminal telephoned his co-conspirators to release Baron unharmed.

He was dumped without payment on the outskirts of Paris. Eight more kidnappers were arrested and sentenced to long terms of imprisonment.

But for the time gained by the police in the long negotiations, it would not have been possible to solve this case without the payment of ransom.

# 13

# Protection for the Family

WHEN FACED WITH the threats to his person, the Executive will be most concerned with the safety of his wife and children. This worry is likely to affect his performance and efficiency. It is therefore necessary for the organisation to simultaneously take steps to strengthen the security arrangements for the family members. This is a bit more complicated than the steps we have delineated for the executive. The quality of family life may be affected. Security should also take into consideration the educational, cultural and emotional needs of the family. It is not uncommon for the miscreants to kidnap the family members as secondary targets to bring pressure for the payment of ransom. The responsibility for the protection of the family is that of the executive. How can he go about this job?

## 1. Education

The family members should be educated about the threat without creating panic.

## 2. Adherence to Security Rules

Family members should be explained in detail the significance of the various preventive and protective drills laid out for the residence like discretion, telephone discipline, avoidance of set routine, alarm systems, emergency drills, safe havens, fire arms, etc.

### 3. Training of Children

Children are apt to exaggerate and boast. This tendency should be slowly modified. Grown up children should be told not to keep undesirable company and bring their friends into the home. Younger children should be advised to avoid strangers and not take lifts in their cars nor accept any eatables or presents. They should be advised to move in pairs, avoid lonely roads and stay at a friend's house and call for the parents to pick them up in case they are held up somewhere. They should know how to summon help in an emergency.

### 4. Keep Track of Movements

Children should be advised to leave details of where they are going and where they could be contacted in an emergency. They should be briefed that emergencies may be simulated and they should not leave the school with unknown persons. School authorities should also be briefed about the apprehensions and requested not to allow the children to leave the school without proper authorisation.

### 5. Resistance

In case of assaults, children should be advised to resist and shout for help. The slogan is 'Kick and Holler'

### FBI Guidelines for Protection of Children

Safeguards for Children

1. Keep the door to children's room open in the night so that you can hear unusual noises.
2. Be certain that children's room is not easily accessible from outside.
3. Never leave young children at home alone or unattended and be certain that they are left in the care of responsible, trustworthy person.

4. Instruct children to keep the doors and windows locked and never admit strangers.
5. Teach children as early as possible, how to call the Police. Teach them to contact Police if they find prowlers or strangers around the house or attempting to get in.
6. Keep the house well lit if it becomes necessary to leave the children at home.
7. Instruct the servants not to let in strangers under any circumstance.
8. Schools as well as parents should ensure that there is always adult presence when children are at play.
9. Advise children to:
   a) Travel in groups or pairs.
   b) Walk along heavily travelled streets and avoid isolated areas.
   c) Refuse automobile lifts from strangers and refuse to accompany strangers on foot.
   d) Immediately report to the Police of anyone molesting or annoying them.
   e) Never leave home without telling parents where they will be and who will accompany them.
   f) Play only in the school or community play ground.

## Nine Rules for Children

1. Never let strangers into the house.
2. Avoid strangers. Do not accept lift or gifts from them.
3. Tell your parents where you are going and how to reach you.
4. Learn how to call Police in an emergency.
5. Travel only on main thoroughfares.
6. Inform parents if you see strangers near your house.
7. Play only in School or community play ground.
8. Give a false name if ever asked by a stranger.
9. Never discuss the security systems you have in your house with any one other than family members.

## Special Advice for Women

1. Be aware of criminals trying to snatch your purse. Keep it close to your body and hold it with both hands.
2. Do not carry all your credit cards in your purse.
3. Do not flash large amounts of cash.
4. Before entering your car check visually that it has not been tampered with.
5. Always park in a well lighted area.
6. If the car breaks down raise the hood and trunk and remain inside the car till police arrives on the scene.
7. Do not pick up hitch hikers of either sex.
8. Walk only in well lighted streets.
9. Stay in the middle of the platform/sidewalk.
10. If followed, be prepared to run towards the area where there are many people. Inform the policeman immediately.
11. When boarding late night, sit near the driver.
12. When in an elevator/lift, stand close to the control panel. If attacked, press the alarm.
13. Do not keep valuables or keys in the coat pocket.
14. Always inform the office security, if you are working late.
15. If attacked or molested, scream as loud as possible. Strike at the vulnerable part of the assailant. Gouge eyes with thumbs, scratch with finger nails, bash temple, nose and Adam's apple with the shoe or elbow. Kick in the groin or testicles. Grab fingers and bend backwards sharply. Report the incident to the Police immediately.
16. Never stand alone in the nights on the bus stands. Take shelter where there are people and come to the bus stand just in time.
17. If abducted, fight and throw your things from the vehicle, scream loudly. Attract attention.

# 14

# Personal Protection Personnel - Bodyguard

In protecting Political Dignitaries, Personal Protection Personnel have distinguished themselves. The classic instance is that of the attempted assassination of President Reagan in 1981. Entire world saw on the Television, how the Personal Protection Personnel, disregarding risk to their lives, saved their Dignitary. The word Bodyguard originated from the concept that these personnel guard their charges with their bodies. In other words, they physically shield their charges and interpose their bodies between the danger and their charges. Thus, they are mentally prepared to give their lives to save the lives of their charges. In the area of Protection of Executives, deployment of Bodyguards have been very few and there are no cases of valour as witnessed in the case of President Reagan. The reasons are not far to seek. The governmental protection systems have some inherent built in advantages, which enable the Protection Personnel to give their professional best. Consequently, the image of a private bodyguard is one of a Hulk ready to charge and crush anything suspicious approaching the protected person. The movie image is also one of unthinking brute. In real life, brain scores over the brawn.

In business environment, the Top Executive seldom has time to plan and implement his own preventive and protection programmes. A security professional assigned as bodyguard can oversee this aspect and provide the necessary inputs for the Executive. Risk Reduction then takes place. The Personal

Protection Personnal also helps in collection, analysis and evaluation of the threat intelligence and identifying threat factors. He can also make advance visits and preparations for the Protectee's engagements. Depending on the threat assessment, the personal protection personnel should take his position along with his protectee, so that he can effectively interpose between the threat and the protectee.

## Basic Guidelines

A bodyguard undertaking protection responsibilities for the first time with a new protectee, should keep the following in mind:

1. ***Familiarisation*** : He should familiarise himself with the personal habits, routines and the social and business obligations of the protectee;
2. ***Rapport*** : At the earliest, he should establish a close rapport with his charge. Without the willing cooperation of the protectee, he cannot achieve anything;
3. ***Past History*** : He should get briefed and study all aspects of security which made it necessary for the protectee to hire a bodyguard;
4. ***Personal Profile File*** : He should prepare carefully, an Executive personal profile file for the protectee(Pl. See Ch.VII for the Format );
5. ***Reconnaissance*** : He should undertake an personal reconnaissance of the route, car, workplace and the residence to locate chinks in the protection system;
6. ***Anti-sabotage check*** : He should personally undertake anti-sabotage check of the vehicle and the office room as often as possible and on a regular basis;
7. ***Work Procedure*** : He should discuss and determine the parameters of his work so that no misunderstanding occurs between him and the protectee. Often, the protectee would like to utilise body guards as personal aides, thereby restricting their availability maneuverability in an emergency;
8. ***Medical History*** : He should discretely ascertain the

medical history of the Protectee and collect such information as may be necessary to deal with a Medical emergency; and

9. ***Communication*** : He should establish in consultation with his protectee, signals and other communication processes that are to be employed in case of an emergency.

## Professional Conduct and Operating Procedures

1. ***Self Discipline***: The bodyguard should always remain alert and remain fully focused on his professional duties. He should never get himself immersed in the goings on around him.
2. ***Never leave the Protectee***: Under no circumstances, a bodyguard should leave his protectee alone and without protection. Miscreants will create deliberate diversions to take away the bodyguard from the scene.
3. ***Vary routine***: It is the responsibility of the bodyguard to vary the routine of the protectee often to introduce an element of surprise.
4. ***Taking Position***: The bodyguard should place himself between the protectee and the direction of the greatest risk or threat.
5. ***Eschew unrelated tasks***: The bodyguard should resist the temptation and make a conscious effort to avoid getting engaged in unrelated tasks.
6. ***Background Study***: The bodyguard should collect and study material on all the incidents involving threats to the Business executives in general and the protectee in particular. All these are to be studied in depth to locate the weak points in security systems and to plug the loopholes.
7. ***Detection of Surveillance***: The bodyguard should take special efforts to detect surveillance at the residence, routes and the office of the protectee.
8. ***Not to reveal Mission*** : The bodyguard should guard against the tendency to discuss with all and sundry his

duties, his specialisation and display of his weapon etc.

9. ***Threat will come from outside*** : The bodyguard should develop the second habit of always looking around for danger. Often the bodyguards look at their protectee. They should remember that the threat will come from outside and not from the protectee himself.
10. ***Remove the Protectee from the scene of trouble*** : The bodyguard should always remove the protectee from the scene of any trouble. He should not engage himself in any fight to prove to his protectee his capabilities. It should be remembered that often these incidents are created as a prelude to kidnapping.
11. ***Maintain Cool*** : The bodyguard should never get provoked and keep his cool under trying circumstances.
12. ***Watch for hands*** : The bodyguard, while moving in the crowds with his charge should always watch the hands of those trying to get close to the protectee. Remember the adage: "Eyes never killed anyone, but the hands have".
13. ***Warn the Protectee*** : The bodyguard should establish a communication or signal system with his protectee, to warn him of dangers.
14. ***Precede the Protectee*** : On all occasions the bodyguard should precede the protectee.
15. ***Respect Privacy :*** The bodyguard should respect the privacy of the protectee. He should not intrude on the personal affairs of the protectee, unless they have a security implication.
16. ***Maintain Confidentiality*** : The body guard should maintain strict secrecy about the itinerary, engagements etc. of the protectee.
17. ***Remain Close*** : When accompanying the protectee on travels, the bodyguard should remain close to the protectee at all times.
18. ***Establish Liaison*** : The bodyguard should know and establish liaison with Police and other local authorities to enlist their support in case of an emergency.
19. ***Front Seat*** : During road journeys, the bodyguard should

take his position in the front seat of the car. He should discretly watch the rear view mirrors for vehicles following or proceeding ahead to notice any surveillance or attempt to box-in.

20. ***Body cover*** : Whenever the protectee gets in or out of the car, the bodyguard should remain near the open door to provide a shield. He should look out for any suspicious movements.
21. ***Bearing*** : The bodyguard should conduct himself with dignity and decorum. He should be pleasant to people and attempt to merge with the environment.
22. ***Dress*** : The body guard should dress conservatively and should not put on flashy dresses which may attract unnecessary attention to himself.
23. ***Abjure alcohol and stimulants*** : The bodyguard should abstain from imbibing alcohol and stimulants. For the same reason he should not take sophoric medicines while on duty.
24. ***Physical Condition*** : The bodyguard should constantly train to be in the best of physical condition.
25. ***Low Profile*** : Consciously cultivate to remain low profile.
26. ***Dedication*** : The bodyguard should remember that the protectee has entrusted his life in his hands. It is more than a matter of employment. It is a matter of trust. He should live up to that.

## Hiring of Bodyguards

Unlike the western countries, we, in India, do not have any training facilities to train bodyguards. Mere police and military background will not make one a good body guard. Nor employing local toughs, former Boxers and Wrestlers would help. Selection should be made very carefully. People with special branch, intelligence, NSG, SPG backgrounds should be preferred. A sound mind resides in a sound body. Pre-employment medical examination including eye test should be mandatory. Psychological tests to detect unsavoury traits should be undertaken.

It is always preferable to employ a full time bodyguard from your own organisation. Never employ a contract security bodyguard.

## Fire Arms

India has strict regulations regarding possession and use of the guns. Normally bodyguards will not have weapons. If the protectee has a weapon, it may be possible to enter the name of the bodyguard in the license as a retainer. In that case, he can legally carry the weapon of the protectee and in the event of a life and death situation, use the same, exercising his right of private defence to save a life.

## Instances where Presence of Bodyguards could not Save the Protectee

### Case of Hans Martin Schleyer

Hans Martin Schleyer, Chairman of Mercedes Benz, was an important personality in West Germany and he was being targeted by terrorist groups for kidnapping. The authorities had provided him with official protection. His house had round the clock police presence and he was escorted on road journeys by three armed police officers in an unmarked car. On the day of the kidnapping, as usual, Schleyer left his office followed by the armed escort. His car was on the way blocked by another vehicle and in effort to avoid collision the driver swerved the car and hit the curb. In the meanwhile, the escort car rammed into the main car. Terrorists , who were waiting at the ambush site , surrounded the escort car and killed all the three police officers, before they could react. Schleyer was kidnapped and later killed when the Government refused to concede the demands of the terrorists.

### Case of Mr. Aldo Moro

Mr. Aldo Maro, a respected leader and former Prime Minister

of Italy was on the 'Hit List' of the Terrorists and he was provided with official protection. A bodyguard was always travelling in the front seat of his car and an escort of police officers followed the car. On the day of the occurrence, Aldo Maro's car was suddenly blocked by another vehicle and the driver applied sudden brake. The escort car rammed into the main car. The terrorists who were waiting in ambush, killed the driver and the bodyguard. They also opened fire at the escort party killing two instantaneously and the third one was shot by a sniper when he attempted to open fire. Maro was kidnapped and later killed.

# PART II

## Diplomatic Protection

# 15

# Protection of Diplomats

INTERNATIONAL TREATIES and Conventions demand that the host country protect the Diplomats and the Property of Diplomatic Missions. Any attack on the Diplomats, conveys the impression that the host country is not in a position to safeguard them and places that country in an embarrassing situation, causing loss of face in the international community. Therefore, when a diplomatic mission is threatened or a diplomat has been taken hostage, the host country is in a great hurry to settle the matter, much to the advantage of the miscreants. Further, the kidnapping of diplomats makes big news and gives publicity to the organisation of the miscreants. Thus, kidnapping of diplomats derive their effectiveness as weapons of political pressure, propaganda and publicity. Often, it gives an insignificant group of miscreants, international publicity. Thus, Diplomats have become the prime target for kidnappings.

Hostage taking in Diplomatic Missions has also become an international pastime among the miscreants. Bombings and Arsons follow in the number of incidents. A two pronged attack is necessary to ensure the safety of the diplomats. The first is the action by the host government and the second is the action by the diplomats themselves.

## Governmental Action

As Diplomats are kidnapped mostly for deriving political

advantages and rarely for monetary gains, actions against diplomats have been largely from terrorists and other politically violent groups. Over the years, number of incidents are increasing. To put an end to this trend, Nations have taken tough measures like 'No Negotiation Policy', ' No Asylum Policy', 'Extradition of wrong doers' etc. In addition, measures aimed at maximising the risks for the kidnappers and minimising the rewards to them have also been taken. As a corollary to this policy, host states provide exhaustive security protection measures to the diplomats and the Missions. Special emergency response teams have been constituted. Public declaration that no negotiations will be held with the terrorists have been made. Elaborate plans have been drawn up to deal with problems of negotiations, communication with the terrorists, coordinating the actions of the host government and the Government of the diplomat, and a well defined crisis management effort.

A detailed study reveals that most of the diplomats kidnapped belonged to Industrialised Democracies of the West and the United States, followed by Middle East countries. Diplomatic kidnappings and Hostage taking and barricading occurs mostly in Latin America; bombings and assassinations take place in the Western Europe and the Middle East

Demands made by the terrorists pertained to release of imprisoned comrades, publication of manifestos in the mass media and in a few rare instances demand for ransom money.

## Action by Diplomats

Diplomats should follow the principles detailed for the personal protection of the Executives. The practical problem often arises in the fact that diplomats are also concerned with collection of information, which requires them to travel widely and often hobnob with undesirable characters. Diplomats also shun the local Law Enforcement agencies as they fear that in the garb of providing security, the latter may start surveillance on them. Thus, often diplomats themselves complicate matters by withholding full cooperation to the local authorities. The fact however remains that any action to neutralise local threats will have to be undertaken by the local authorities and they could be ignored only at the peril of the diplomats. Thus, in addition to taking all preventive actions themselves, diplomats should keep up close liaison with the local police or the Diplomatic Protection Service and frankly discuss with them the threats and take their advice for preventive actions and implement them in letter and spirit.

## Action by Diplomatic Missions

A study of the Hostage taking and barricading instances reveal that these were made possible by the Missions themselves not taking adequate security precautions. Since the Mission premises is considered to be a foreign territory, local police will not enter the same, unless invited. It is in the interests of the Missions to fully associate the local police while making arrangements for big events like National Day celebrations and other major events. It should be realised that many VIPs who are facing threats to their personal safety will be attending these functions and it is the responsibility of the hosts to ensure their safety. Since they are in a foreign country, the Missions should enlist the cooperation of local authorities to ensure this. The latest instance of hostage taking in Peru at the Japanese Ambassador's residence proves this fact. There was hardly any security arrangement. Traffic regulation is not protective arrangement nor can it prevent hostage taking. Often, miscreants enter the Mission premises as visitors. Visitors control is very lax in almost all Missions. While it is necessary to keep a friendly profile to the visitors, certainly arrangements can be made to segregate the visitors from sensitive areas.

# 16 Case Studies

## Kidnapping of British Ambassador in Uruguay

Sir Geoffrey Jackson was the British Ambassador in Uruguay in 1971. He realised that he was under surveillance and based on the then prevailing trends, he suspected that he may be kidnapped. He noticed that in the Park opposite his house, there was always a family picnicking. Almost daily, his vehicle was being followed by Scooters with young couples. His security staff noticed that while the couples changed, the two wheelers were the same. Later heavier vehicles started cutting in apparently testing the reaction of the driver. Everyday there was always a young couple standing with a scooter in front of the Embassy. Sir Jackson was certain that he is going to be kidnapped. He visited the Foreign office in London along with his wife and apprised the officials about his premonitions. A decision was taken that in the event of his being kidnapped, no concessions will be offered to the kidnappers and none will be asked for from the Government of Uruguay.

Sir Jackson decided that neither he nor his bodyguard would carry any weapons. He followed sensible preventive measures like varying the route etc. and the kidnappers found it difficult to detect a pattern to plan action. Ultimately, on January 8, 1971, Tupamaros mounted a major operation with multiple teams, blocked the roadway and created diversions and with a van rammed the vehicle of Sir Jackson and kidnapped him. This took place in a narrow road. He was held for eight months in two different locations in filthy conditions.

As earlier agreed, the family refused to entertain any plea from the terrorists and both the British and Uruguayan Governments refused to concede the demands of the terrorists. Sir Jackson maintained his dignity and composure through out the ordeal and won the sympathy of the general public. The kidnappers found that they are unlikely to get any concessions and any harm done to the victim will rebound on them. Taking the excuse of a Prison escape, where some terrorists escaped, they announced success and released Sir Jackson.

## Seizure of the Us Embassy in Tehran

Three thousand Iranian Militants raided the Embassy of the United States at Tehran on November 4, 1979 and took a large number of hostages. Two weeks later, thirteen women and Blacks were released keeping only 50 hostages. The demands were rhetorical and without substance. US appealed to the Iranian Government to ensure the releases of the hostages, which was favoured by the Iranian Prime Minister but he was overruled by the Supreme leader Ayatollah Khomeini. Instead of terminating the hostage situation, the Security Forces abetted and aided the miscreants. The Prime Minister resigned in disgust. The hostages were put to severe indignities. As the hostage situation prolonged, the US Government attempted military intervention on April 24, 1980 and the operation flopped due to defective logistics support. Ultimately using the good offices of the Algerians, the hostages were released on January 20, 1981.

The hostages spent 444 days in detention.

## Seizure of the Dominican Embassy in Bogota

On February 17, 1980, Dominican Embassy in Bogoto had a well attended reception. Opposite the Embassy was a University playing field. 25 members of the terrorist group M 19 assembled there as sportsmen. As the Reception was in progress, on a signal from a conspirator inside the Embassy, the referee blew the whistle and the 25 terrorists whipped up their concealed weapons, attacked the Embassy killing one guard and seized 75 hostages including 14 Ambassadors. They released non-diplomatic staff and one sick Ambassador but held the rest for two months. Initially they demanded release of 300 prisoners and payment of a ransom of US$ 50 million.

The Columbian government refused to negotiate. A consortium of businessmen from the countries of the hostage Ambassadors raised US$2.5 million as ransom and paid the same. The terrorists and the hostages were flown to Havana. The entire negotiations received world wide publicity for the terrorists for two full months.

## The Seizure of Iranian Embassy in London

In April 1980, six anti -Khomeini terrorists seized the Iranian Embassy in London and took 26 hostages. The terrorists wanted their demands to be broadcast over the BBC .This was done on the fourth day and on the fifth day five sick and a pregnant hostage were released. The terrorists wanted safe passage out of England. This was against the policy of the British Government. On the sixth day the terrorists killed one hostage and threatened to kill one every 40 minutes, if their demands were not met. Taking this threat seriously, the Embassy was stormed by the elite counter-terrorist force, the SAS, and five terrorists were shot dead and the sixth was captured. He was later sentenced for murder. One hostage died in the cross fire and all others were rescued.

# PART III

## Protection of Political Executives

# 17

# Sources of Threats

Political Executives face threats to their lives from the following sources.

## Enemy Agents

Hostile nations attempt to create political instability and conditions of chaos in the target country by organising political assassinations through their intelligence agencies. This is achieved either by creating a network of agents from political dissent groups or by sending in their own intelligence operations. History is full of such instances. The task of locating and neutralising the enemy agents is that of the National intelligence agencies.

## Persons Opposed to the Political System

In any political system governing a country, there are dissidents, who sincerely believe, on the basis of their ideology, that the country would benefit by adopting a different system. Thus, there are people who oppose democracy and would like to opt for a dictatorship. Extreme right-wing groups, Fundamentalists, and religious groups would like to usher in a theocratic set up for the country. Since their advocacy is unpopular, they tend to adopt assassination as the means for effecting a change in the political system.

## Political Opponents

In any political system, the aim of the opposition is to seize political power. To achieve this, the opposition, continuously, denigrates and criticises the leaders of the ruling group/party. They exaggerate and highlight the faults, omissions and commissions of the ruling party. While saner elements in the opposition take these as propaganda gimmicks, volatile elements in the opposition have come to notice in the past for having fallen a prey to these intense hostile propaganda and resorting to violence against political personalities, resulting in their death.

## Persons affected by the Policies of the Government

Economic, social and development policies of the government are formulated with maximum good for maximum number in view. Thus, these policies leave out a section of the population from the benefits and also adversely affect a section of the people and deprive them of their economic and social rights and often their privileges enjoyed over a long period of time. Such deprivation, creates wide spread resentment among these groups and many of them lend their support and resources to those planning to cause harm to the political executive.

## Mentally Unstable Persons

There are people, who are mentally ill and affected with a phobia, which could be termed as "VIP COMPLEX". In their disturbed mental condition, they nurture imaginary grievances against the political executives and go to any length to cause harm to them. Many assassinations have been carried out by such individuals. None of them had any valid grievance against the political personality whom they had assassinated.

Unlike an individual business executive or an ordinary citizen, the Political Executive cannot point out the threat to his personal security to the authorities concerned. What has been indicated above is the general category of the sources of threat. The precise source of danger cannot be pin pointed. Any harm befalling a Political Executive will have National and International repercussions and consequences. By the very nature of their role and duties to the public, it is not possible to advise the Political Executive to take preventive measures by curtailing physical exposure. They are required to constantly meet the people, often without prior appointment and in public places, to be seen at massive rallies and public functions, and any ostentatious protective arrangement is likely to make them unpopular.

Thus, keeping the threats mentioned above in view and in the absence of specificity, protection arrangements are required to be done in a very comprehensive manner.

# 18

# Principles of Protection

As has been seen in the previous chapter, there are many threats for the Political Executive and it is not possible to pinpoint them. The Political Executive is also required to maintain his public exposure and constantly meet and have discussions with the members of the Public. Then how can we ensure his safety? Following principles will take care of the same.

## Access Control

Since the threat in most of the instances will manifest through human beings, it is necessary to ensure that those who get access to the Political Executive is a known person authorised to meet him or the one who has been vouschafed to be a non-threat by some one known to the authorities. Thus, the basic premise of all protection arrangements will be to ensure that ***no unauthorised or unvouschafed person has access to the Political Executive.*** Strict access control alone will take care of the unknown danger.

## Concentric Circles

To prevent the unknown danger from reaching the Political Executive and to enforce strict access control, the protection arrangements are made in the form of concentric circles. Thus, to reach the Political Executive, the threat will have to pass through many barriers or obstacles. These could be in the form of physical, electronic, technological and human elements.

## Non-Display of Arrangements

To have the required effectiveness, the arrangements should not be displayed. They should be low key and often camouflaged from public gaze. This will ensure that there is an element of surprise to the threat when it reaches the proximity of the Political Executive. Further, high profile protection arrangements are likely to affect the public image of the Political Executive.

## Cooperation of the Protected Person

It is essential to have the confidence of the protected person and to enlist his cooperation in the implementation of the arrangements. Every arrangement proposed will have to be carefully evaluated and analysed from the angle of its likely impact on the political fortunes of the protected person. Nothing should be done to mar his public image. Everyone values his life. Political Executive is no exception. Once the need for the restrictions or special procedures are explained to him and he sees their importance, the protectee will cooperate with his protectors.

## General Order is Important

Presence of popular political leaders generate wild enthusiasm among their followers resulting in disorderliness and chaos during receptions and other celebrations. These are the occasions being keenly watched by the miscreant, to take advantage of and to cause physical harm to the Political Executive. Therefore, there is imperative need to maintain general order around the protected person.

## Facets of Protective Arrangements

There are three well defined spheres of protective arrangements:

### Intelligence

All information about the potential threats are to be collected routinely, studied, collated and analysed to locate the sources of threats. These threats are to be kept under constant scrutiny and observation. This information should be updated on a continuous basis. Data on all denigrating and vituperative references to the protected person, telephone threats, hate mail and unfavourable media reports are all to be compiled. Whenever, the protected person makes his travel plans, these data are to be consulted to determine on the nature and quantum of protective arrangements to be made. They would provide the information for the likely motive for violent actions against the protected person.

### Indirect Defencive Measures

These are aimed at removing possible risks from different sources. These would include, screening of mail and packets received by the Protected Person to eliminate Letter Bombs and Parcel Bombs; careful check of the car, office and residential area to detect explosives; ensuring the purity of food and victuals and drinks to eliminate poisoning; screening of visitors; and security vetting of domestics and others who will be constantly near the Protected Person.

### Direct Defencive Measures

Direct defencive measures are meant to confront the threat as and when it manages to reach the protected person. These would include, alarm systems at the residence and office; bullet proof cars; body guards, escorts during journeys etc.

## Integrated Chain

All the three facets are complementary to one another and form an integrated chain. Success of the arrangements would depend upon these three working in cohesion and unison. Even if one fails, disaster will be the result.

## Planning Protective Arrangements Determining the Threat Quotient

The intelligence data should be studied to determine the "Risk Quotient". By a process of logic and based on past experience, each piece of information should be evaluated to determine in the given situation and circumstances, which of the threats are presently more serious than the others.

## Locating Likely Avenues of Attack

This is a method of self appraisal of the existing protective arrangements. Having determined the risk quotient, an exercise should be undertaken to see how the potential threat would breach the existing arrangements. This could be done better, if a team could plan an actual attack in a simulated situation and another team is entrusted with the task of protection. This type of war games will simulate the interest among the protection personnel.

## Organize Surveillance over Well Known Threats

All well known threats are to be carefully kept under surveillance to detect any hostile moves from them against the protected person.

## Prepare a Blue Print

Having examined the weaknesses or the chinks present in the existing arrangements, a blue print should be prepared to create a series of obstacles or concentric circles to cover the protected person. Due allowance should be given to the possibility of human failure. In other words, sufficient backup for various arrangements should be built into the blue print. This has to be shared on the basis of 'Need to Know' with the concerned.

## Implementation

Successful implementation of the blue print would call for briefing of the personnel who would operate the various segments of the same, their understanding of the rationale behind them and their dedication. It should be remembered that mere numbers do not enhance the effectiveness and value of arrangements. More the manpower, the more likely to be dilution in responsibility and accountability. Careful selection of personnel, their mental and physical make up and their capacity to make quick and effective judgements are some of the factors which should be taken note of.

## Contingency Plans

Remember Murphy's Law. If things can go wrong, they will. Prudence dictates that one should have alternate plans ready if the planned arrangements go awry. These would include alternate routes, emergency evacuation of the protected person, medical aid, spare modes of transport, etc. One should not invent non-existent possibilities while preparing contingency plans. These plans are to be kept confidential and should be known to only few individuals.

## Constant Review

Protection arrangements are to be reviewed on a daily basis constantly to locate the chinks in the armour. It would be desirable to constitute a one-man team to critically review the arrangements on daily basis to point out the flaws. Lessons are to be drawn from near-misses and narrow escapes.

## Zero Defect Situation

In protection work, one will be judged by his mistakes and not by his past performances. Therefore, one should aim for a zero defect situation at all times. Critical self appraisal, quick thinking and pragmatism will help in this. Despondency, bravado and fatalism will not deliver the goods. Protection to be perfect, demands hard, honest and sincere work and dedication and sacrifice.

# 19

# Arrangements for Specific Situations

## Residence

SPECIAL CARE SHOULD be taken to prevent direct physical attack, through strengthening of perimeter security arrangements and to screen all visitors. In terrorist infected areas, the arrangements should extend beyond the compound to detect attack with missile type weapons. Sufficient number of armed personnel should be available to act as an Emergency Response Team. Alarm systems, communication systems to summon additional reinforcements etc. should be catered for. Secondly, steps are to be taken to eliminate the risk of sabotage. Physical features of the residence are to be checked to locate points vulnerable for sabotage and suitable steps are to be taken to eliminate them. Thirdly, steps are to be taken to prevent mischief through arson, explosives, poisoning etc. Arrangements to cater for emergencies caused by natural and man made causes are to be planned.

## Journeys by Car

All precautions suggested for the safety of the business executive will apply equally to Political Executives. Threats from the vehicle, driver's inability to respond to a crisis, route, high-rise buildings, crowds on the route and the cross traffic are to be eliminated. An escort with armed personnel and a bullet proof car are essential for Political Executives. A personal bodyguard should travel in the front seat of the car at all times. Adequate arrangements to meet vehicle breakdown, medical emergencies etc. should be available.

## Train Journeys

Sabotage to the tracks, tampering with the signals to create a collision, sabotage to the special coach, mischief through food and drinks, access to the protected person by unauthorised individuals, danger from servicing personnel etc. are to be considered and steps taken to guard against them.

## Air Journeys

Protective arrangements should cover the security of the air strip or runway; security of the aircraft; vetting of air and service crew; purity of food and drinks; security of the baggage to prevent sabotage; standby arrangements etc. If the Political Executive is travelling by a commercial airliner, in addition to the above, threat from co-passengers and the possibility of Hijacking are to be considered and eliminated. Ancillary arrangements for fire fighting, medical emergencies etc. are to be available.

## Public Function

Closest liaison with the local police and security authorities should be maintained. General protective arrangements and proximate protection arrangements are to be available.

It may be seen, that we have only indicated broad outlines of protective arrangements as it is not desirable to spell out the details in an open publication, as it is likely to be of help to the miscreants. We are sure, that the discerning reader will understand our difficulties and appreciate the limitations placed on the author, in the larger interests of the safety of Political Executives.

# 20

# Case Studies of Assassinations and Attempts

AN ANALYTICAL study of the assassinations and attempts at assassinations will help the reader to understand the importance of various measures stressed in the previous chapters and to draw lessons from the failure of the protective arrangements in these instances. It is not our intention to pass any judgement on the professional competency and efficiency of the organisations entrusted with the protection work in those cases. We are discussing only some of these cases as full documentation is available in open published material. Each one of these cases is of special nature and the problems involved were many. We will be giving the facts of the case in a bare narrative and indicate the areas of failure and leave it to the reader to devise ways and means to prevent such occurrences.

'Wisemen learn from others' experience and not so wise from their own ' says an adage. Let us be wise.

## Political Leaders of the World Assassinated while in Office in the Past Five Decades

(Assassination of Political leaders out of office and other important personalities are not included)

April 1947 — Gen Aung San, Dy.Chairman of Ruling Junta of Burma, killed by political rivals.

| | |
|---|---|
| August 1949 | President of Syria, Hosni Zaim, killed by the Army. |
| July 1951 | King Abdullah of Jordan, killed by extremists in Jerusalem. |
| October 1951 | Prime Minister of Pakistan, killed in a Public Meeting. |
| July 1958 | King Faisal of Iraq, killed in Military coup. |
| September 1959 | Prime Minister of Ceylon, killed by a political conspirator. |
| September 1961 | President of Dominican Republic, Rafael Trujillo, assassinated in power struggle by political opponents. |
| November 1963 | President of the United States, John F.Kennedy, assassinated by a political extremist in Dallas. |
| January 1965 | Prime Minister of Iran, Hassan Ali Mansur, shot dead. |
| January 1966 | Prime Minister of Nigeria, Abubakar Tafawar Balewa, died in coup. |
| September 1966 | Prime Minister of South Africa, Hendrick Verwoerd, stabbed to death in Parliament House by the assassin. |
| November 1971 | Prime Minister of Jordan, by Palestinians in a Hotel. |
| October 1973 | Prime Minister of Spain, in an explosion. |
| March 1975 | President of Chad, Ngarta Tombolbaye, died in Army Coup. |
| August 1975 | President of Bangladesh, Sheikh Mujibur Rehman, shot dead in Army coup. |
| February 1976 | Head of State of Nigeria, Gen. M.Muhammad shot dead in an abortive coup. |
| April 1978 | President of Afganistan, Muhammad Daoud, killed in coup. |
| June 1978 | President of Yemen Republic, Lt.Gen. A.H.Ghashmi, killed by petrol bomb. |
| October 1979 | President of South Korea, Park Chung Hee, shot dead. |

| | |
|---|---|
| April 1980 | President of Liberia, William Tolbert, shot dead in Military coup. |
| May 1981 | President of Bangladesh, Zia-ur-Rahman, shot dead in Military coup. |
| August 1981 | President and Prime Minister of Iran, killed in a bomb blast. |
| October 1981 | President of Egypt, Anwar Sadat, killed by soldiers. |
| September 1982 | President-elect of Lebanon, Bashir Gemayel, killed in bomb blast. |
| October 1984 | Prime Minister of India, Mrs.Indira Gandhi, killed by her own bodyguards. |
| February 1985 | Prime Minister of Sweden, Olof Palme, shot dead by an unknown assailant. |
| May 1993 | President of Sri Lanka, Premadasa, killed by a human bomb. |
| November 1995 | Prime Minister Of Israel, Yitshak Rabin, killed by an extremist. |

## Attempt on the Life of President Andrew Jackson of USA - January 1835

**Facts**

President Jackson was participating in a funeral procession in the capital. Richard Lawrence, an Englishman, came close to the President, took out a Pistol and pointing at the chest of the President, fired. Though the percussion cap had exploded, it did not ignite the powder. Lawrence threw the Pistol down and took out another one and fired. This also failed. In the meantime, he was overpowered by those around the President and handed over to police custody.

President's escape was truly providential. Had the pistols worked, at such close quarters death was inevitable.

Investigations revealed that Lawrence was mentally ill and was suffering from an illusion that he was the king of England and the USA was one of his possessions. He had unsuccessfully tried to meet the President thrice and had also solicited monetary help from the Staff of the President. The Judge remanded him to mental custody and he finally died in the mental asylum.

**Lessons**

1. People with 'VIP COMPLEX' are dangerous. His earlier approaches to the President should have been properly investigated and he should have been sent to a mental asylum as a preventive measure.
2. At all times strict access control should be maintained around the protected person.
3. Had concentric circle arrangements been present, Lawrence would have been stopped at a distance from the President.

## Assassination of President Abraham Lincoln - April 1865

**Facts**

While watching a theatrical show on April 14, 1865, President Lincoln was shot, in the back of the head, by a famous actor, John Wilkes Booth. The President succumbed to his injuries. Booth fled the scene on a Horse kept ready for escape and he was tracked down and shot dead by the soldiers.

Investigations revealed that Booth was an ardent believer in the dominance of the 'South' and he had hated the policies of President Lincoln. He also disliked his personality. He wanted to take revenge on the President for the 'injustices' done to the 'South'. On the day of the occurrence, he found the bodyguard absent from the Presidential Box and taking cover of the curtains, he stealthily reached behind the President and shot him.

Booth had a well known bad mental history. He had a strange streak of melancholia. He had an obsession that he would gain immortality by doing an act which would go down in history. He had violent tendencies. He was once arrested for publicly denouncing the President and the State policies but was let off after he pledged allegiance to the Union.

**Lessons**

1. The fact that the President would be in the same theatre as Booth, who was well known for his anti-President views, should have prompted the authorities to keep Booth under observation and strengthened arrangements around the President.
2. Selection of Personal Protection Personnel should be thorough to eliminate personnel with weaknesses for Wine and Women. They should be closely supervised. In this case the bodyguard deserted his post to have a glass of beer, which enabled Booth to kill the President.

## Assassination of President Garfield of USA - July 1881

**Facts**

On July 02, 1881, President Garfield was walking on the Platform of Baltimore Railway Station to board a train. He was shot in the back by Charles Guiteau. A second shot was also fired and it did not hurt the President. The President was hospitalised and he died in September 1881.

Investigation revealed that Guiteau was suffering from many illnesses and was mentally unstable. He was having a delusion about his importance. He published a pamphlet supporting President's candidature during the elections and he was convinced that this was responsible for President's election. He wanted to be adequately compensated for this. He pestered the President and the Department of State with many petitions, sponsoring himself for prestigious diplomatic assignments. He also felt that the policies of the President are dividing the

Nation. He decided to kill the President as he felt that he was ordained by the Divine Powers to do so.

During the trial, it came to notice that Guiteau bought a Revolver and a box of cartridges with borrowed money and wanted to kill the President on June 18, itself. When he saw the frail looking Mrs.Garfield clinging to her husband, he changed his mind. He came to know of the President's proposed train journey from the newspapers. He surveyed the Railway Station and hid himself in the Ladies waiting room on the Presidential path. He even paid a visit to the jail and ascertained that conditions there are comfortable for him. He even hired a carriage to take him to the prison after the assault. After completing all these preparations, he hid himself in the Ladies waiting room on the fateful day. As the President passed the place, he came out, followed the President and fired at him from the rear. The second bullet just grazed the coat sleeve of the President. Guiteau was taken into custody immediately.

At the trial, the plea of insanity was rejected and he was sentenced to death. He did not exhibit any remorse or repentance and till the end he maintained that he was divinely ordained to kill the President.

**Lessons**

1. Security officials should reconnoiter the area to be visited by the Political Executive well in advance to detect suspicious persons lurking in the area.
2. Personal Protection Personnel should always look around for anyone following the Protected person and to intercept him.
3. Guiteau has been pestering the President and the State Department for favours. His activities should have been kept under watch.

## Assassination of President Mckinley of USA - September 1901

### Facts

On September 6, 1901, President McKinley was greeting the public individually at the Guilded Hall of Music, Buffalo. Public lined up for that purpose and were enthusiastically shaking hands with the President. Leon Gorlogoz, a young American worker was in the line, with a handkerchief covering his hand. When he reached the President, he shot him twice with the revolver concealed under the handkerchief. President succumbed to the injuries on September 14, 1901.

Investigations revealed that Leon did not have any history of mental illness or violent tendencies. He read about the assignation of King of Italy by a poor weaver. He felt that no one should enjoy as much power as the President of USA and felt that his assassination would help the poor. He kept the project to himself.

A week before the assassination, he bought a revolver and ammunition. He reached the hall much before the President and found the same as being well guarded by the Police and Secret Service Agents. He joined the line of people to greet the President. He noticed that a man with a bandaged hand in the line ahead of him was being affectionately greeted by the President. He took out his Revolver and covered the same with the handkerchief. The two Secret Service Agents near the President presumed that Leon had an injury and one of them assisted him in moving forward. When the President was in front of Leon and was about to greet him, Leon shot the President twice, even as the Secret Service Agent's hand was still on his shoulder. He was immediately taken into custody.

At the trial, Leon dispensed with counsel and pleaded guilty. He was sentenced to death.

### Lessons

In protection work, one should never take things for granted.

In this case, adequate arrangements were there. President lost his life because the two secret service agents presumed that Leon had an injured hand. Had they exhibited little curiosity and observed carefully, they could have detected the weapon. In protection work, hands are always to be watched.

## Attempt on the Life of Mr. Theodore Roosevelt - October 1912

### Facts

Mr. Theodore Roosevelt was running for the Presidency for a third time and quite a few in the country disliked the idea. The Presidential candidates were not being given any protective arrangements in those days.

John Schrank, an emigrant from Bavaria, was living with his uncle and whose establishment was closed during the time Roosevelt was the Commissioner of Police. He also felt that two term Presidency is a sacred American tradition and Roosevelt was violating the same by standing for the third time. He also dreamt that the ghost of President McKinley had asked him to kill Roosevelt to avenge his death.

Presidential candidate was staying in a Hotel in Milwaukee. Schrank took his position near the entrance of the Hotel on the Street. As Roosevelt came out and waved to his admirers and was about to board the car, Schrank shot at him through the crowd. The bullet hit Mr.Roosevelt on the right chest. Its impact was reduced due to the thick wad of campaign speech in the coat pocket and a metal spectacle case. The bullet entered the chest and remained lodged there through out his life.

### Lessons

This incident highlights the need for keeping the alighting and embarking points clear of all unauthorised persons.

## Assassination of Archduke Ferdinand of Austria - June 1914

### Facts

Archduke Ferdinand of Austria was the heir-apparent to the Hapsburg Empire, which consisted of many small nationalities clamouring for self-determination. The Slavs in the South detested the Empire and for the extremists amongst them, the Archduke personified the denial of freedom, autonomy and unification and he deserved to die to further their cause. Motivated thus, six Slavs led by Gavrilo Princip, decided to take the opportunity of the visit of Archduke to Sarajevo to inspect some military establishments, to assassinate him. They took their positions on the VIP route. As the carcade came near, one of the assailants asked the policeman on duty to point out the Archduke, which he readily obliged. The assailant hurled a grenade on the Protected person, which missed and rolled under the escort car and exploded. Later in the day, the Archduke wanted to visit the military hospital to see the wounded escort personnel and it was decided to take a safe route. The pilot car took a wrong route and after some time tried to reverse this carcade to the correct path. The assailants were tracking the Archduke and when they noticed the confusion, Princip managed to reach the main car and shot dead the Archduke and his wife. It was claimed later that one policeman actually saw Princip raise the revolver and rushed to disarm him but was prevented from doing so by two fellow conspirators.

## Assassination of Archduke Culminated in World War I

### Lessons

1. This incident portrays how chaotic conditions help the miscreants.

2. When last minute changes are made, it is necessary to brief all concerned. The Pilot officer obviously did not know about the change in the route.
3. Brief the police personnel on the route to watch for suspicious people approaching the protected person.

## Attempt on the Life of President Elect F.D. Roosevelt - February 1933

### Facts

President Elect Franklin Delano Roosevelt was addressing a meeting of his supporters in a Park in Miami on February 15, 1933. As soon as he concluded his speech and the crowd was dispersing, Zangara, a brick layer of Italian origin stood on a chair and opened fire from a revolver. Though Roosevelt escaped unharmed, five people around him received serious injuries, of which the Mayor of Chicago died after a few days in Hospital. Roosevelt escaped unhurt, because the chair on which Zangara was standing was unsteady and two of the audience reportedly clutched his hand holding the revolver in an attempt to disarm him. Hence, his bullet missed the target.

Investigations revealed that Guisseppe Zangara was of poor origin and felt capitalists were responsible for the plight of the poor. He felt that the assassination of Kings, Presidents and Prime Ministers was a noble task. He set out to kill the King of Italy but was unnerved by the Royal Bodyguards. He wanted to kill President Hoover, but he was in Washington and the cold climate did not agree with him. He was waiting for the arrival of an important person in his area.

On the fateful day, Zangara reached the park well in time and found all seats were taken. He remained at the periphery and as the meeting was dispersing, advanced forward, climbed a chair and started shooting at Roosevelt. His chair was unsteady and he could not take proper aim.

During the trial Zangara never expressed regret for his action but expressed disappointment that he could not kill Roosevelt. He was electrocuted.

**Lessons**

1. Zangara is an example of a person with a 'VIP COMPLEX'. Such individuals require careful watch.
2. The need to be attentive at the conclusion of the functions, especially when the crowds start dispersing, has been highlighted in this episode.

## Assassinatin of Lord Moyne, British Resident of Egypt - November 1944

**Facts**

Lord Moyne was the Resident British Minister in Egypt in 1944. He was branded as Pro-Arab by the Jews and was hated by them. His residence was a vast villa with sprawling lawns and shrubbery. On November 6, 1944, as usual, Lord Moyne was returning from office for lunch with his Secretary and the A.D.C. Two Israeli youth, who wanted to kill Lord Moyne were observing his daily routine very carefully for many days. On the fateful day, they took their position near the main gate. Though they were noticed both by the Secretary and the A.D.C., the officials did not take any action. As the car was winding its way through the long drive way, the youth vaulted over the wall and positioned themselves near the portico. As the driver opened the door for the Lord to get down, one youth covered the driver and the other shot the Lord from the other side of the car. The assailants were captured by a police patrol later.

**Lessons**

1. The need to cover the alighting point with protection arrangements is highlighted in this incident.
2. The need to vary the daily routine.
3. The need for the personal staff to be alert, when they notice the strangers.

4. When the car stops, the Personal Security Officer or the A.D.C. should get down first and survey the area and provide physical cover to the protected person.

## Assassination of Gen. Aung San of Burma - April 1947

**Facts**

Gen Aung San was a popular and dynamic leader of Burma. He was holding a cabinet meeting on April 19, 1947 in the Government palace. Four armed men in Army fatigues, burst into the council chambers and opened fire with automatic weapons. Aung San and seven other ministers died in the shooting. A security guard of one of the ministers was also killed.

Gen Aung San had a serious political rival in U Saw. In all departments of politics, Aung San worsted U Saw. Having failed to defeat his rival in the political game, U Saw, hatched a conspiracy to kill the General and enlisted the help of few radical youth. As soon as the cabinet assembled, on a prior signal, four of the assailants dressed in Army Jungle fatigues, drove up to the building in an Army vehicle and burst into the council chamber and opened fire with automatic weapons. Investigations unearthed the conspiracy and the conspirators were hung.

**Lessons**

1. Always check the identity of the people having access to the Protected person. Mere uniform is not enough for identification.
2. Access control was absent in this case.
3. Bodyguards of the Protected persons should be available in the proximity to intervene.
4. Intelligence about the conspiracy was lacking.

## Attempt on the Life of President Harry S. Truman - November 1950

### Facts

President Harry S.Truman was staying in the Blair House in Washington in November 1950. Two Puerto Rican Youth tried to shoot their way into the Presidential Apartments by indiscriminately firing with small arms. They were shot at by the Security personnel. One died on the spot and the other was seriously injured. President and family remained unhurt.

Torresolo and Collazo, the Puerto Rican youth, wanted to do something spectacular to draw the attention of the world to Puerto Rico. After arming themselves with small arms, they reached the Blair House, temporary residence of the President and split into two and approached the house steps by opening rapid fire. Naturally, the fire was returned by the security personnel resulting in the instantaneous death of Torresolo. Collazo was seriously wounded.

At the trial, Collazo justified his act as patriotism. He was sentenced to death for the murder of the policemen in the shoot out. President commuted the sentence to life imprisonment.

### Lessons

This incident shows that determined assassins will not stop short of achieving their objective at the risk of losing their lives. The main principle in the protection is to deny access. Once the assassin comes close to the Protected Person, he can be stopped only at great cost.

## Assassination of Prime Minister of Pakistan October 1951

### Facts

Prime Minister of Pakistan was addressing a Public Meeting

of over 50,000 people organised by the ruling Muslim League party at Rawalpindi. Suddenly, from the crowd, a lone assassin fired two shots rapidly at the Prime Minister from close quarters. The dignitary received fatal injuries in the chest and abdomen. The assassin was overpowered by the crowd. A Police officer shot at him repeatedly with a revolver and the crowds taking the cue, lynched the assassin. Investigations disclosed that the assassin Syed Akbhar was a religious fanatic, who dabbled in occult experiences. He considered that the Prime Minister with his progressive policies was un-islamic and he should be killed.

Investigations further revealed that the organisers refused to heed to the advice of security authorities in making arrangements for the function and the crowd was allowed to be very close to the dignitary. This assassin was within 15 feet from the dignitary. The Prime Minister was speaking from a low podium of 4 feet height. There was no proximate protection arrangement near the podium.

**Lessons**

While making protection arrangements when the dignitary is present at large gatherings, sufficient distance should separate the crowds from the dignitary. The dignitary should be in an elevated position compared to the crowd. Proximate security arrangements should be available around the dignitary to provide a human shield in an emergency. Security personnel should watch the crowds to detect unusual movements and to warn the dignitary of the danger.

## Assassination of S.W.R.D Bandaranaike, Prime Minister of Ceylon - September 1959

**Facts**

Mr. S.W.R.D.Bandaranaike, Prime Minister of Ceylon, was a forceful political personality with strong views on men and matters. His style of functioning and many of his policies were not to the liking of the conservatives and the Buddhist Clergy. He was very proud of his popularity and dispensed with security arrangements at his residence except for a solitary armed sentry at the gate. He used to receive large number of visitors at his residence. Powerful conservative elements wanted to do away with him and selected a Buddhist Monk Somarama Thero as the assassin. Somarama was a quack and he was about to lose his practice due to the reforms in medical practice being brought by the Prime Minister. Further, in Ceylon, Buddhist Monks are venerated and Somarama can have unquestioned access to the Protected Person.

On the fateful day, Somarama armed with a .45 revolver concealed in his robes, took his place along with other visitors at the Prime Minster's residence. When Bandaranaike came out greeting everyone and on seeing Somarama bowed in reverence before him. Simultaneously, Somarama whipped out the revolver and shot at the Prime Minister.. Though injured, Bandaranaike ran inside the house. He was chased by the assassin and was shot again thrice. Bandaranaike succumbed to his injuries the next day. Investigations unearthed the conspiracy and three conspirators were sentenced to death. Somarama was hanged and the other two were given life sentence on appeal.

**Lessons**

1. Need for screening visitors.
2. Need for a bodyguard to be always present near the protected person.
3. Need for intelligence to unearth conspiracies.

## Assassination of President John F. Kennedy - November 1963

**Facts**

On November 22, 1963, President Kennedy was driving in an open car in a motorcade in Dallas. Mrs. Kennedy and the

Governor of Texas were also with him. As the car was passing in front of a multistoried building known as Texas School Book Depository, shots rang out in quick succession. Both the President and the Governor were seriously injured. President Kennedy succumbed to the injuries within an hour of the attack.

Investigations revealed that the shots were fired from the sixth floor window of the building by Lee Harry Oswald with a powerful Italian Rifle. Background investigation disclosed that the assassin had a deep rooted antagonism towards all American authorities and had earlier emigrated to Soviet Russia and married a Soviet woman. He had great admiration for Cuba and he disliked the US policy towards Cuba. He unsuccessfully tried to assassinate a high ranking military officer before assassinating the President. Unfortunately, before the investigations could be concluded, Oswald was shot dead in the court premises by a right-wing extremist. Killing of Oswald opened the floodgates for speculations and conjectures. Till today, controversy is going on in USA regarding the actual motive behind the assassination and who killed President Kennedy.

**Lessons**

1. Never use an open car for the Political Executive's travels.
2. Take care of all high rise buildings and roof tops. Watch out for snipers.
3. Oswald's history was known to local police. He was a potential threat to Political Executives. Yet, he was not kept under watch.
4. Warren Commission, which enquired into the assassination, found that the security authorities displayed lack of coordination and cooperation and there were lot of gaps in the arrangements.
5. The commission also pointed out that the Secret Service Agent driving the Car did not have proper reflexes and a quick reaction from him would have saved President Kennedy.

# Assassination of Henrick Verwoerd, Prime Minister of South Africa—September 1966

## Facts

On September 6, 1966, the Prime Minister of South Africa was in his seat in the Parliament and was reading some papers. He was stabbed to death by a Parliament messenger. Tsafendes, a non-white from Mozambique had a bad mental history. He managed to secure the post of a temporary Parliament messenger. It is usual to employ temporary staff during the sessions of Parliament. The temporary personnel are generally used in minor errands and only permanent staff are utilised inside the House. Tsafendes nurtured a hatred for Mr.Verwoerd as he thought he was personally responsible for all the ills of Mozambique and that he was working in league with the Portuguese.

On the fateful day, Tsafendes brought two long knives with him to the Parliament house and concealed them inside his uniform. As the Prime Minister was in his seat reading some papers, Tsafendes, approached him as if to deliver some message. No one took any notice of him as he was in the uniform of the messenger. On reaching the Prime Minister, he whipped out the knives and repeatedly stabbed him four times. He was overpowered by other members of Parliament. The Prime Minister succumbed to his injuries. Tsafendes was committed to a mental asylum till death.

## Lessons

1. Need for proper verification of antecedents and character of people who will work in the close proximity of the protected person.
2. Strict access control.
3. Need to induct security personnel in exclusive surroundings like Parliament to deal with emergencies.

## Attempt on the Life of Polish President at Karachi – November 1970

### Facts

The President of Poland was on a State visit to Pakistan. On November 1, 1970, he arrived in a special plane at Karachi Airport and was being ceremonially received by Pakistan dignitaries. As the visiting President and his entourage were greeting Pakistan dignitaries and were moving up the reception line, a catering van of the Pakistan International Airlines, bore on them at great speed and mauled down those assembled. The President, who was pushed aside by a quick thinking security officer, survived. His deputy foreign minister and three Pakistanis died on the spot and many others were seriously injured.

Investigations revealed that the driver of the killer van, Feroze Abdullah was a religious fanatic and was plotting to cause harm to the Pakistani Political leaders. On the fateful day, he was off duty. But as he was in P.I.A. uniform, he could get access into the airport. He found a catering van standing with the ignition keys on and without anyone in attendance. He got into the van and slowly moved upto the VIP side of the airport. Armed guards and the security personnel on duty thought that the van was proceeding to 'Service' the VIP aircraft. As soon as he neared the nose of the aircraft, Abdullah speeded up and mauled down the reception line. His intention was to kill Pakistani dignitaries. He had nothing against the Polish President.

### Lessons

1. Need to prohibit vehicle movements in the area where there is movement of Political dignitaries.
2. Need for security personnel not to take anything for granted.
3. Need to create an 'Out of Bounds' area at the time of ceremonials.

4. Need to have control over vehicles parked in the vicinity.

## Assault on the Prime Minister of U.S.S.R. Ottawa - October 1971

### Facts

Prime Minister Kosygin of U.S.S.R. was on a week long visit to Canada in October 1971. On October 18, 1971 after a meeting with the Prime Minister of Canada, he was scheduled to drive down to the Hotel. He actually got into the car. As the weather was fine, at the suggestion of the host, they both wanted to walk down the distance, which was only 100 metres. As both the Prime Ministers started walking down, a large contingent of T.V. and Media persons also followed them. There were many Canadian and Russian Security personnel around the dignitaries. As they proceeded for a short distance, a young man from the crowd, rushed at the Soviet Prime Minister, put his arm around his neck and shoulders and pushed him to the ground. Within seconds, the youth was overpowered and the dignitary was helped to his feet.

Investigations disclosed that the assailant was an Hungarian immigrant with strong anti-Soviet views. He could have caused serious harm but was interested in only registering his protest against the soviets.

Violent demonstrations from Jews and other anti-Soviet elements were expected during the visit and elaborate security arrangements were made.

### Lessons

1. Lack of alertness on the part of security authorities. They should watch out for miscreants and not concentrate their attention on the VIP. The threat will come only from outside.
2. Whenever the Protected Person walks on foot, a large crowd will follow. Security personnel should form a tight cordon around the dignitary.

3. The bodyguard should always remain close to the dignitary to provide a shield in case of sudden attacks.

## Assassination of Prime Minister of Jordan in Cairo - November 1971

### Facts

Prime Minister of Jordan was in Cairo to attend the Arab Defence League meeting. He was staying in Sheraton Hotel, Cairo. After attending the meeting in the pre-lunch session, he was returning to the Hotel at 3-45 p.m. on November 28, 1971. As he was about to enter the Hotel, four Palestinian youth, who had earlier taken their positions in the Hotel lobby, fired at him with automatic weapons. The Prime Minister, the Foreign Minister and an Egyptian security officer were seriously injured. The Prime Minister succumbed to his injuries.

Investigations revealed that the four young men belonged to the terrorist group, the 'Black Hand of September'. They were angry at the strong action taken by the Jordanians against Palestinian commandos in September 1970 and held the Prime Minister personally responsible for the action. They wanted to assassinate him. On the fateful day, armed with automatic weapons suitably concealed, they entered the Hotel and had refreshments in the Cafeteria. They quietly moved to the lobby. They saw the Saudi delegation arriving at 3-35 p.m. and knew that the Jordanians would follow. They took their positions near the entrance. As soon as the Jordanian delegation entered the Hotel, assassins opened fire with their automatic weapons. They were later captured.

The threat to the Jordanian delegation was well known. Elaborate security arrangements were made. A block of 17 rooms were booked for their use and as many as 15 Jordanian security officers were in the delegation. Egyptian authorities also made elaborate security arrangements. Yet, everyone forgot to keep the Hotel lobby under observation and secure the alighting point.

**Lessons**

1. Secure the alighting and entry points.
2. The arrival and departure are very important and crucial events from security point of view. Therefore maximum vigil should be maintained at these times.
3. Do not allow the crowds to gather or loiterers to be present at the main entry point.
4. Always provide a separate entry and exit points for the Protected Person away from the main lobby and common entrance for the other guests.

## Assault on the President of West Germany - October 1973

**Facts**

On October 19, 1973, the President of West Germany was addressing a meeting of the Association of Young Entrepreneurs at Augsberg Congress Hall. After he completed his speech, a person walked upto him and hit him on the face. The dignitary fell down. The assailant was overpowered and a search revealed that he had on his person a long knife.

Investigations revealed that the individual had a mental history and had come to notice for intemperate utterances against the dignitaries. He was considered to be a security threat by Federal authorities. Though he was spotted in the crowd by the police, no action was taken either to remove him or keep a watch over him during the function.

**Lessons**

1. Need to keep watch over security threats.
2. Need to remove suspicious persons from the proximity of the Protected Person.
3. Writers of threatening letters should be kept under watch.
4. Need for better coordination between various agencies.

## Assassination of the Prime Minister of Spain - December 1973

**Facts**

Prime Minister of Spain was in the habit of attending Mass daily in a Church on his way to office from his residence. He was very punctual. Taking advantage of the regularity of the movements, some of his political opponents wanted to assassinate him on his way to the office from the church. One of the conspirators hired a basement of a house on the route claiming to be a sculptor. He tunneled his way under the road and placed powerful explosives below the road. They were set to be exploded from outside. A red mark was painted on a wall and as the car passed the mark, the priming device was triggered, setting off the explosives right under the car. The explosion threw the car up five stories high and created a crater of 30 metres wide. The conspirators had also placed a car full of explosives near the site of explosion, as a matter of added precaution. This car was set to explode synchronously with the main charge. The Prime Minister, his bodyguard and the driver died on the spot.

**Lessons**

1. Vary the routine.
2. Change the route often.
3. Need to run an advance car and watch for unusual things on the route. The redmark should have been noticed by the Police patrols.
4. Census and periodical verification of people on the main VIP route.

## Attempt to Assassinate the President of South Korea - August 1974

## Facts

On August 15, 1974, the President of South Korea was delivering his ceremonial address at the National Theatre in connection with the opening of the Liberation Day Celebrations. He was addressing the people from behind a bullet-proof lectern. His wife was on the podium seated at some distance from him. As the President was delivering his speech, a member of the audience, ran down the aisle towards the podium with a revolver in hand and fired thrice. The President ducked behind the B.P. lectern and escaped. His wife was fatally injured. The assailant was overpowered by the security officials.

Investigations revealed that the assailant was a political extremist with views diametrically opposed to that of the President. He remained in exile in Japan for a few years as he could not accept the political dispensation in the country. He read the novel 'The Day of the Jackal' and was inspired by it to commit the assassination of the President. He arrived in Seoul from Japan on August 6, and took up residence in an expensive Hotel. He visited the National Theatre area earlier and thoroughly studied the security arrangements. On the fateful day, he arrived at the venue in an expensive car and in the presence of the security officers, gave a very large tip to the driver. His car did not have special parking label. He entered the lobby and waited. When questioned by the security authorities, he said he was from the Japanese Embassy. No one bothered to ask for his diplomatic I.D.card nor notice that his car did not have Diplomatic number plate. He was allowed to stay. Originally, he intended to kill the President in the lobby. He could not get a chance. He quietly moved into the Hall and took his seat 35 metres away. During the proceedings, he whipped out the revolver, ran towards the podium and fired three shots.

The Security arrangements for the function were very thorough. Admission was by invitations, which the invitees were asked to produce at the entrance. Guests were asked to wear distinctive ribbons, sent in advance, on their lapels. The assailant had neither. Moreover, as he ran towards the Podium, a full 35 metres, none of the numerous security officers present stopped him. They were watching the function. The President was saved by the bullet proof lectern.

### Lessons

This is a classic case of human failure. On paper, all arrangements were there. But the implementation was a total failure. The need for proper briefing of the security personnel, frequent supervision by the senior officers are called for. In this case, the security personnel failed to display any alertness or agility.

Note: Some months later, this dignitary fell a victim to a bullet, when during a dinner party with high-ranking officials, there was heated discussions followed by a gun fight and one of the bullets killed the President accidentally.

## Assault on the Prime Minister of Japan – June 1975

### Facts

On June 16, 1975, the Prime Minister of Japan was attending the funeral service of a former Prime Minister. He was waiting at the front entrance of the Nippon Budoken Hall for the arrival of the ashes. A group of Press Reporters were standing near the Prime Minister. The assailant, Fudayasa, reached the Prime Minister from behind the Press group, and punched him twice on the nose, shouting " Nuclear Non-Proliferation". The Prime Minister fell down and his spectacles were broken. The assailant was immediately overpowered and his search revealed that he was carrying a knife with a 13 inches blade and a letter addressed to the Prime Minister suggesting that he should commit suicide. Having reached the dignitary, the assailant could have easily killed him, if he wanted to do so. Investigations revealed that the assailant was the Secretary General of an ultra rightist organisation opposed to the

Government. He had over 50 arrests to his discredit. While on his way to the funeral hall, he was accosted by the police. Yet, he was let in. There were four bodyguards and fourteen plainclothes security personnel around the Prime Minister, when the assailant struck.

**Lessons**

1. Keep all suspects under watch and do not allow them to reach the Protected Person.
2. Security personnel should concentrate on their job and be alert. They should not get absorbed with the events and goings on around them.
3. This is classic case, to prove that large number of security personnel will not assure protection. A lone miscreant got the better of eighteen security personnel.

## Assassination of President of Bangladesh – August 1975

**Facts**

As a result of political conspiracy hatched by politcal elements opposed to the President of Bangladesh and Junior level Army Officers, on the night of August 15, 1975, armed soldiers led by Junior Officers burst into the official residence of the President of Bangladesh and mercilessly killed him and some members of his family. The Security Guards posted at the Residence could not react to the swift events that unfolded. The conspirators installed a friendly Government of their choice. They were well rewarded and no worthwhile punitive action was taken against them.

**Lessons**

The danger to the lives of the protected persons due to conspiracy amongst defence forces should be always kept in mind while planning security arrangements. Sufficient fire power should be available at the residence of protected persons to meet sudden onslaught by armed groups. More than defending against such attacks, plan should be available to quickly evacuate protected person to safety.

## Attempt to Assassinate Prime Minister Rajiv Gandhi of India Rajghat, Delhi, October 2, 1986

### Facts

Every year, on October 2, VIP assemble at the Samadhi of Mahatma Gandhi at Rajghat to offer prayers and to pay homage to the Father of the Nation. In 1986 also, in accordance with this practice, the President of India, Prime Minister Rajiv Gandhi, almost the entire Council of Minister and other VIPs were present at Rajghat. A lone Gunman, fired thrice at the Prime Minister Rajiv Gandhi at different intervals from a well chosen hiding place. He failed to kill the VIP as he was using a poor quality country made weapon.

Prime Minister Rajiv Gandhi arrived at Rajghat at 6.55 A.M. on October 2, 1986 as he was proceeding on foot towards the Samadhi, a sharp sound was heard. The VIP kept on walking. The bullet, which should have struck the Prime Minister was later found embedded in a Flower Bed just behind the spot where the Prime Minister was standing when the sound was heard. As prayer service was going on, security forces tightened their vigil and started combing the entire area but could not detect the hidden assassin.

After the prayers, as the President and Prime Minister were coming out of the Samadhi at 8.00 A.M. and proceeding towards their vehicles, another shot rang up. Security men scurried all over the place with guns at the ready. They could not locate the assassin. As VIPs reached near their cars a third shot rang out and injured two persons walking slightly behind the Prime Minister. Two of the security personnel also received pellet injuries.

By this time, the security personnel had seen smoke emanating from the creepers surrounding a concrete canopy. They quickly surrounded the area and started shooting into the foliage. A young man, stood up on the roof of the canopy with his hands raised above his head and shouting that he wishes to surrender. He was taken into custody.

Investigations revealed that the assassin Karam Chand, who was bearing grudge against Rajiv Gandhi for his inaction in respect of victims of 1984 riots and on the Punjab Problem, occupied the roof of the canopy, which was at a height of 10 feet from the ground level on September 25, 1986 and has been camping there. An intelligence report dated September 27, 1986 which was circulated to all the Security agencies gave specific information that a youth, who has been a victim of anti-Sikh riots of 1984, will approach the VIP area in the garb of a gardener and would hide himself in the bushes to cause harm to a VIP. As this information was classified as unverified, it was not taken very seriously. While standard checks were carried out at Rajghat none bothered to check the roof of the canopy where the assassin was hiding. Incidently this was the only possible hiding place for any one in that area. Yet security forces ignored this obvious place.

**Lessons**

(1) All intelligence reports should be treated with all seriousness and thorough follow-up action should be taken to eleminate the risks suggested therein.
(2) Security checks, to be effective, should be carried by more than one agency independent of each other, in a methodical wave formation. This will ensure that anything missed by one agency would be recovered by another one.
(3) As soon as the first shot was heard, the worst should have been presumed and VIP should have been taken back to the safety of his bullet proof car. He should not have been allowed to proceed on foot till the area has been completely checked. Similarly, the route for the return

journey of the VIPs should have been changed.

## Attempt to Assassinate Prime Minister Rajiv Gandhi of India, Colombo, Sri Lanka, July 30, 1987

### Facts

As the visiting Prime Minister of India, Rajiv Gandhi, was inspecting a ceremonial Guard of Honour on July 30, 1987 a Sailor from the Honour Guard slashed at him with the butt of his rifle. As the visiting VIP saw the sudden movement and quickly ducked, he received the blow only on the shoulder. Had be been hit on the head, he would have died on the spot.

Investigations revealed that the sailor W.V. Rohana, has a reputation for bad temper and unbalanced mind. He had hatred for Rajiv Gandhi for having supported LTTE in the earlier years and for imposing Peace Acccord on Sri Lanka. He harboured a feeling that the Prime Minister of India was personally responsible for the ethnic strife in Sri Lanka. He had never made a secret of his feelings. Everyone knew about his antipathy towards Rajiv Gandhi. He was not in the original detail but was selected to replace some at the last moment. He detested his duty as he was to undergo many rehearsals and hard work. He had decided to teach a lesson to Rajiv Gandhi, During interrogation he was unrepentant but stated that he only wanted to hit the Indian Prime Minister but never wanted to kill him if he had that idea of killing him he would have used bayonet against the VIP.

### Lesson

Any one having access to a protected person should be carefully screened. Mere membership of defence of police service should not be taken as a clearance for goodwill. Examples of the assassinations of Aung San and Prime Minister Indira Gandhi should reveal that these VIPs met their fate at the hands of military and police personnel. It is necessary to keep the protected person at a distance from Honour Guard.

## Assassination of Prime Minister of Israel Tel Aviv, November 4, 1995

### Fact

Mr. Yitzhak Rabin, Prime Minister of Israel was working hard to bring peace to his country and towards this end was actively pursuing a policy of friendship towards Palestinians. This was not to the liking of Right-wing elements in Israel. Prime Minister was constantly receiving threats to his life and his security cover was also enhanced.

On November 4, 1995, Prime Minister Rabin was addressing a Peace and Anti violence Rally in Tel Aviv. At the conclusion, he was shot twice by a Right-wing extremist youth with a 9mm pistol. Mr. Rabin died a few hours later.

Investigations revealed that a Right-wing conspiracy to murder Mr. Rabin was in full swing for the past many months and Police Informer gave precise and full information about the likely profile of the assassin and the methodology as early as June 15, 1995. Unfortunately, the security services did not act on this information as they believe that a Jew will not assassinate an Israeli VIP. The assassin actually tried to kill Mr. Rabin twice earlier than November, 1995 could not get a suitable opportunity. Over confidence and casual approach to threats from Right-wing elements resulted in this tragedy. There was no check on the assassin as he moved towards his target as he was wearing the mandatory cap of an orthodox jew. Though many security personnel were present none intercepted him.

### Lessons

This assassination is result of faulty and inadequate appreciation of information received from informers. A protection personnel should have an open mind while dealing with security threats and examine all information closely and take suitable preventive actions. Every piece of information should be treated as correct and serious preventive steps will have to be taken.

## Attempt on the Life of President Ford – September 1975

### Facts

On September 5, 1975, President Ford was walking on the grounds of the Capital flanked by the Secret Service Agents. Several hundred people greeted him from behind the barricades. President Ford went near the crowd and started shaking hands. Suddenly the President and a secret service agent saw a hand with a gun coming up from the rear row. The agent shouted "gun", and grabbed the weapon and the woman holding it. Other agents provided a protective cover and removed the President from the spot. Alertness of security personnel saved the President.

Investigation disclosed that the woman was a cult member and had two months earlier sent a warning that if President Ford continued to be in office, there would be bloodshed. It was also reported that when she aimed the gun at the President, she shouted that " the country is in a mess and this man is not your President" The gun did not fire as the chamber was empty though there were four bullets in the magazine. This error in loading the weapon perhaps, saved the life of the President.

### Lessons

1. Always watch the hands and be alert. Never take the protected person too close to the crowds.
2. All threatening utterances like the one made by this woman should be carefully investigated. Had this been done, the mental state of this woman would have come to notice and perhaps, she would have been under surveillance on the fateful day.

## Assassination of Prime Minister Indira Gandhi of India – October 1984

### Facts

In the eighties, Sikh militancy was at its height and they were indulging in Terrorist acts all over India. Many armed Terrorists took shelter in the premises of the Golden Temple in Amritsar. An operation to dislodge them was launched by the security forces, which resulted in the death of many terrorists including their leaders and also considerable damage to the Holy Shrine. This caused deep resentment among the devout Sikhs and this was exploited by the Terrorists. Sikh militants blamed the Prime Minister personally for the damage done to the Holy Shrine and for launching the security operations. They wanted to assassinate her. Since the security arrangements around the Prime Minister were elaborate, they hatched a plan to subvert security personnel of Sikh faith. They succeeded in winning over two of them.

On October 31, 1984, Prime Minister Indira Gandhi was moving from one building to another in the residential complex. As she was on the pathway, two Sikh security personnel opened fire at her from close quarters, one with a handgun and the other with an automatic weapon. The Prime Minister was riddled with bullets and died shortly thereafter.

On hearing the shots, armed security personnel rushed to the spot and overpowered the assailants. Later one of them was fatally wounded, when trying to overpower the guards.

Investigations revealed an extensive conspiracy. Conspirators were arrested and tried and sentenced to death. It was further revealed that there were glaring systemic deficiencies in the security system protecting the Prime Minister.

### Lessons

1. Never take anything for granted in security work. There

were reports about the strong feelings of hurt among the Sikhs. Yet, nothing was done to ascertain whether these feelings had affected the Sikh security personnel.

2. There was a system of keeping the off-duty activities of security personnel under watch. This was not enforced in respect of personnel working in the residence of the Prime Minister.
3. There was a suggestion from the highest security professionals to remove the Sikh security personnel from proximate protection duties. This was overruled by the Prime Minister herself but no action was taken by the senior bureaucrats to convince the dignitary about the need for the same.
4. One of the assailants switched duties to be at a vantage point to kill the dignitary. This change was not noticed.
5. At the time when the assailants opened fire, no bodyguards or other security personnel were present near the dignitary. They were perhaps lulled into the belief that in a secure environment there is no need for close protection.
6. Even after the event, there was no control over security personnel by senior supervisory officers and the death of one of the assailants deprived subsequent investigations, valuable clues.

## Assassination of Olof Palme, Prime Minister of Sweden – February 1985

### Facts

Prime Minister Olof Palme was a very popular and unassuming leader and security arrangements for him were minimal. On the fateful day, he attended theater with his wife and as is his wont, sent away the personal security officers. After the show, he was walking home hand in hand with his wife. An unknown assailant suddenly appeared and killed him.

**Lessons**

1. Popularity of a dignitary has nothing to do with security arrangements. More popular a dignitary, greater are the risks as there would be many political opponents, jealous of the same and hate him for that. Security arrangements should be strictly based on the threats. At the time of the assassination, Europe was having a rash of terrorist activities and murders were taking place with sickening regularity. There was thus need to strengthen security arrangements for all dignitaries.
2. While the security officers need the cooperation of the dignitary to make arrangements for their protection, they should not accept the decision of the dignitary in operational matters. While security officers should respect the privacy of the dignitary, they should have been present in the theater in an unobtrusive manner and escorted the dignitary home. It is always possible to provide security without affecting the privacy of the dignitary.

## Assassination of President Premadasa of Sri Lanka - May 1993

**Facts**

President Premadasa was participating in May Day celebrations and was travelling in an open vehicle greeting the people. An LTTE terrorist, posing as an onlooker, came on a cycle full of explosives and detonated it in the proximity of the President. In the explosion, including the President many died.

Investigations revealed that the human bomb had infiltrated into the President's household through a servant with many weaknesses. He was familiar to all the security personnel. As he approached the President's vehicle, none stopped him and he was allowed to come near the dignitary.

**Lessons**

1. In the disturbed conditions of Sri Lanka, President should not have been allowed to travel in an open vehicle and general public should have been kept at a distance. The assassin with the cycle bomb should not have allowed access near the dignitary.
2. There was intelligence failure in as much as LTTE was able to infiltrate into the President's household. There were no checks on the activities of the servants in general and particularly on the one addicted to vices. The need to vet servants in dignitary's household is highlighted in this incident.

# PART IV

## Miscellaneous Threats to Business

# 21

# Threats from Special Interest Groups

IN THE PAST TWO decades, threats from well meaning citizens have started affecting Businesses in developed countries particularly, the United States and the West. These are threats from Anti-Nuclear, Animal Rights, Anti-abortion, Anti-development and Pro-environmental groups. Consisting of well placed and respectable citizens, these groups have a fanatical allegiance to their cause and have caused damage to business property and have indulged in abductions. Their tactics border on those of terrorists and they have employed mindless violence to further their cause. They are now being referred to as 'Soft Terrorists'. In India too, we are having such groups giving anxious moments to the law enforcers and business alike. It is necessary for the business executive to know about the threats from these quarters.

These groups generally adopt the following pattern of violence. They start with demonstrations, generally peaceful in nature, to gain publicity to their cause. The next stage is to organise sit ins, dharanas, obstructions and confrontation both with the business management and the Police. If they do not get sufficient publicity and compliance to their demands, they indulge in vandalism by damaging manufacturing facilities with arson, explosives, etc. They then graduate to abduction of Executives and demand acceptance of their demands. Finally, they adopt the classic methodology of terrorists like use of explosives to kill people and damage property, Hostage taking, Hijackings and so on. Often, these groups are infiltrated by political violent elements, who would like to use these platforms to get even with the government or the business organisation. It is not unusual for some hostile business firms to clandestinely fund these organisations, in an attempt to destroy their business rivals.

Anti-nuclear groups have caused lot of damage to facilities in USA, Western Europe and Japan. Animal Rights Groups are particularly strong in the United Kingdom and Western Europe. They have destroyed laboratories, outlets selling animal products and caused personal harm to research scientists and marketing executives. Anti-abortion activists have wrought havoc in USA and Western Europe. Anti-development groups have halted many a development project on the ground that they are disturbing the environmental balance. There have been many cases of abduction of ex-patriate executives to force the stoppage of work on these projects.

Any business organisation likely to become the target of such groups should in the first place constitute a Crisis Management Committee. Secondly, they should take conscious steps to avoid publicity to the threats received from these groups. Thirdly, whenever threats or warnings are received, Police should be informed and full cooperation to them should be given. Emergency drills to deal with bomb threats, arson and activities of sabotage are to be devised and practiced. Executives, who are likely to be affected are to be given additional protection arrangements. Many developmental projects are in remote areas and are beyond the reach of quick response by the police. It is therefore necessary to organise 'Self Defence Squads' with the help of local Police and arm some loyal workers. A panel of competent professionals experienced in dealing with such crisis in the past should be prepared and kept ready and the experts should be called in as soon as an emergency develops.

For obvious reasons, we have not dealt with in detail the incidents that have taken place elsewhere, lest Indian groups may be unwittingly educated by us about their destruction potential. We are sure that discerning readers will understand our deep concern in the matter.

# 22

# Threats to Contaminate Consumer Products

MISCREANTS OFTEN contaminate or threaten to contaminate consumer products with poison and harmful substances in an attempt to extract a ransom from Mega corporations. Often these are indulged in by criminal elements and occasionally by terrorist groups. This method has a poor record of success as the perpetrators invariably get caught. However, the adverse publicity affects the image of the organisation and the marketability of the product and the losses in the market will run into astronomical figures. Thus, there is a tendency on the part of the victims to hush up these cases. Very few cases come to be known and thus the statistics available does not reveal the true picture. We give below some well known cases to enable the readers to understand the strategy involved in dealing with such cases.

## Woolworths of Australia

Woolworths run a large supermarket chain in Australia. They were subject to extortion and bomb threats over a period of three years in 1979-81 and successfully handled them. In the process they had developed an effective and experienced crisis management team.

In November/December, 1979, the Firm received a letter giving a list of products that have been contaminated and have been placed on the shelves of its retail outlets. The letter demanded a sum of Australian $ 500,00 for giving fuller information about the other products that have been contaminated. The Firm was threatened not to inform Police and failure will result in media exposure. Woolworths tested the products listed in the letter and found that the contamination was not serious and withdrew the stocks and informed the Police. The extortioner wrote again and with the help of the police a trap was set but he did not turn up, possibly he knew of the police trap. Media were briefed and requested to keep the matter under wraps, when the extortioner contacted media, he was cold shouldered and he finally gave up the attempt.

Again in October 1980, on an anonymous message, the Security officer in charge of a very big supermarket, located a briefcase in a locker, which contained details of contaminated products and a Note demanding A$ 800,000. Failure to do so will result in placing of contaminated products in 80 more stores. The Firm called a Press conference and announced that all the contaminated products are being withdrawn and new stocks would be placed in the shelves in two days time. Police were also brought into the picture. Nothing further was heard from the extortioner.

On December 17 and 19th, 1980, two stores were damaged in fires caused by explosives. There were no warnings. On December 22nd, a letter was found in a counter warning that more explosives will be set off unless A$ 1 million was paid in cash, gold and diamonds. Four days later, a telephone caller warned the Sydney Stores to be evacuated immediately and a bomb exploded in the toys department shattering the glass. Woolworths immediately offered A$25,000 for anyone giving information regarding these bombs. Media published full details of the extortion message and the code name to be used, which resulted in large number of bogus claims being made for the reward amount. To a further message received on December 31st, 1980, with the full concurrence of the police, the Firm agreed to pay and negotiations started. Agreement was reached on the amount to be paid and the instructions for payment. The money was to be placed in a bag and dropped from a specified wharf in Sydney Harbour. The police located a skin driver and arrested him. Some weeks later a second man was also arrested. Both were put on trial and sentenced to long terms of imprisonment.

Throughout the period in addition to informing the Police, Woolworths hired Control Risks Ltd., a famous consultant firm, and followed their advice meticulously. One could imagine the stress and anxiety of the top management. Yet, they kept their cool and defeated the nefarious designs of the extortioners.

## Coles Supermarkets, Australia

In May 1983, Food Pastes and Eye drops, were contaminated with poisonous substances and placed on the shelves of the Coles Super Market Chain, by an extortioner, who demanded A$500,000 to prevent him from further placing contaminated items. In a series of telephone calls, the extortioner threatened to increase the number of contaminated products but also the ransom amount. Police were informed and posing as Coles Executives, police conducted the negotiations and agreed on payment and delivery procedure. The ransom was to be delivered in a remote mountainous area. An armed man appeared to collect the ransom and when challenged, he opened fire. He was shot dead by the police.

Similar attempts were made in UK and USA in many Super Market chains and in all of them the police were informed and with their active participation in the negotiations and delivery of ransom, the extortioners could be arrested.

Japanese confectionery companies and Supermarkets in 1984 and 1985, also fell victims to extortion racket and they resolutely refused to negotiate or pay the ransom. They had full cooperation of the police but suffered heavy financial losses. Animal Liberation Front of UK laced bottles of Sunsilk Shampoo with Bleaching powder and placed the contaminated bottles on the shelves of retail outlets. This caused lot of damage to Bootes, the company manufacturing Sunsilk shampoo and the product had to be withdrawn from three major cities resulting in huge losses. The same organisation, poisoned Mars chocolate bars in retail outlets with rat poison. Three thousand tons of chocolates were recalled and destroyed, the loss was estimated to be US$ 22.5 million equivalent. The reason given was that the company was using Monkeys in experiments to identify a remedy for tooth decay.

## Tylenol, USA

In October 1982, seven people died in Chicago area after consuming a common remedy Tylenol. Investigations disclosed that they were laced with cyanide. The manufacturers of Tylenol, immediately recalled the product from all retail outlets and wide publicity was given not to use Tylenol. It was found that only the capsules in Chicago area were tampered with and that too at retail outlets. The recall cost the company over U.S.$100 million and loss of sales over U.S.$400 million. The firm reintroduced the product in tamper proof packaging and the public relations exercise cost another U.S.$ 100 million. The modus operandi was repeated by the miscreants in respect of Anacin and Exedrin capsules. The perpetrators could not be traced. One man was arrested and convicted for demanding ransom, but the police believed that he was not the originator of the diabolical plan but one who wanted to take advantage of the situation to make some money.

These incidents would highlight the threats from elements who are on the criminal fringe. No one can anticipate when the danger will strike. The answer is to have a well established Crisis Management (CMT) Team to deal with them as they arise.

# Selective Bibliography


Alexander.Y,and Kilmarx.R,A., *Political Terrorism and Business* (New York,Praeger,1979)

Ayoob. Masasad., The Truth about Self Protection (New York. Bantam Books, 1983)

Cole. Richard,B., ***Executive Security*** (New York, John Wiley,1980)

Clutterbuck. Richard., ***Kidnap and Ransom*** (London. Faber& Faber Ltd 1978)

Cooper. H,H., ***The Hostage Takers*** (London. Paladin Ent. 1981)

Creliston.R,D.,& Szabo.D., ***Hostage Taking*** (Lexington, D.C., Heath.)

Federal Bureau of Investigation *Crisis Reaction Seminar* (February 8-12,1982, FBI, Washington D.C. 1982)

Herz. Martin,F.,(ed.) ***Diplomats and Terrorists: What woks,What Doesn't***. (Washington DC, George Town University, 1982)

International Association of Kidnapping: ***How to Avoid it. How to Survive it.***

Chiefs of Police(1979) ***Clandestine Tactics and Counter Measures.***

Jenkins. Brian, M., (ed) ***Terrorism and Personal Protection*** (Boston & London. Butterworths 1985) Should Corporations be Prevented from Paying Ransom (1974) ***Hostage Survival: Some Preliminary Observations (1976***), ***Embassies under Seige (1980),*** Diplomats on the Frontline (1982) (Rand Corporation, Santa Monica Pamphlets)

Knowels. Graham., ***Bomb Security Guide*** (Boston & London. Butterworths,1976)

Mackenzie. G.,et al ***The Security Hand Book*** (Capetown. Flesch 1981)

Moore. Kenneth., ***Airport, Aircraft and Airline Security*** (Los Angeles. Security World 1976)

Scotti. Antony, J., ***Executive Safety & International Terrorism*** (Englewood Cliffs, NJ. Prentice Hall, 1986)

Subramanian. S., ***Principles of Protection of Dignitaries*** (1980)-out of print.

# Index

Abandoned Mines, 8
Abduction, 3, 4, 7, 36, 39, 60, 165
  Foreign Personnel, 4
  Technicians, 4
Abductors, 86
Action Plan, 14
Air and Foreign Travel,
  Bombers, 47
  Protection, 47
Aircraft,48,51
  Air India 747, 48
  Crew, 51
  El Al, 47
  Executive, 49
  TWA, 48
Airport
  Athens, 48
  Heathrow, 47
  Rome, 47, 48
  Security, 51
  Vienna, 47
Air Travel, 47
  Guidelines, 48-49
Alarm and Warning Devices, 21
Alarm System, 18,95,126
Alarms, 22
  False, 22
  Smoke, 23
Algerians, 113
Alighting Points, 30
Amsterdam, 91
Anacin and Exedrin, 170
Anand Marg, 67
Animal Liberation Front (UK), 169
Anti-missile Technology, 71
Anti-Sikh Riots, 154
Argentina, 84
Armoured Cars, 40
Arrangements, 27
  Access Control System, 29
  Audit, 28
  Checking of Mail Parcels, 29
  Expert, 27
  Guards, 29
  Maintenance Staff,29
  Office Location, 28
  Perimer, 28
  Security, 27
  Telephone, 29

Arson, 74
Assassination and Attempts,
Case Studies, 128
Assassination Attempts
Abraham Lincoln, 131
Archduke, 136
F.D. Roosevelt, 137
Ferdinand of Austria,
136
General Aung San, 139
Garfield(USA), 132, 133
Harry S. Truman, 140
Henrick Venwoerd, 144
John F. Kenneddy, 142,
143
Kosygin, 146
Lord Moyne, 138
Olof Palme(P.M.), 159
President Bangla Desh,
152
President Ford, 157
President McKinley, 134
President Premadasa, (Sri
Lanka), 160
President West Germany,
148
President South Korea,
149-151
Polish President, 145
Prime Minister Indira
Gandhi, 158
Prime Minister Israel, 156-
157
Prime Minister Japan, 151
Prime Minister Jordan, 147
Prime Minister Spain, 149
Rajiv Gandhi,
Colombo, 155
Rajghat, 153-155
SWRD Bandarnaike, 141
Theodore Roosevelt, 135
Astronomical Figures, 9
Attack Dogs, 31
Aung San, 128, 139, 155
Australia, 88, 167, 169
Coles Supermarket, 169
Woolworths, 167-169
Auxiliary Power Units, 28

Baltimore Railway
Station, 131
Bandar Roja, 85
Bandarnaike, SWRD, 141
Baron, Jorge, 84
Baron Empain Case, 93-94
Barriers, Natural and
Structural
Drop Barriers, 28
Fences, 28
Gates, 28
Speed Breakers, 28
Baruah, 67
Bell Captain, 52
Biological Agents
Anthrax, 73
Bacteria, 73
Virus, 73
Black Hand of September,
147
Blackmail and Extortion, 75
Blair House, 140
Blind Folds, 7,8
Bodyguard, 99,104,105,112,
127,131,139,142,159
Basic Guidelines, 100-101
Hiring, 103

Royal, 137
Bomb
Detector, 29
Disposal Squad, 78
Booth, John Wilkes, 131
Boron Brothers, 83-84
Born, Bunge Case Study, 83-85
Buddhist Monks, 142
Buenos Aires, 83
Bullet Proof,
Brief Cases, 31, 71
Car, 42, 43
Resistant Glass, 41
Vehicles, 40
Writing Pad, 31
Burgler Alarm, 21
Business Executive, 3, 12-15, 35, 47, 67-70, 80, 83, 165

Cairo, 147
Call Bells, 18
Call Bell System,
Electronic, 22
Caracas, 85
Case Studies
British Ambassador
Uruguay, 112-113
Seizure of Dominican
Embassy, Bogota, 113
Seizure of Iramian
Embassy, London, 114
Seizure of U.S.
Embassy, Tehran, 113
Cellular Phone, 22, 23, 31
Chemical Agents,
Arsenic, 73
Gas Mask, 73
Gas Suits, 73
Herbes, 73
Lead, 73
Mercury, 73
Micro Organism, 73
Chicago, 170
Chief Security Officer, 76, 78
Civilisation, 3
Compound Wall, 18
Commando Argimiro
Gabaldon, 85
Commercial,
Aircraft, 47
Airliner, 51
Communication,
Letters, 61
Means, 61
Messages, 61
Newspaper Ads.
in Codes, 61
Tapped Message, 61
Telephones Calls, 60-62
Television Network, 61
Communist Block, 70
Concession,
Financial, 4
Political, 4, 5
Publicity, 4
Conspiracy, 140
Conspirators, 158
Contract Killing, 68
Counter-Ambush Drill, 39
Crime, 4
Criminal Gangs, 8, 67
Crisis Management
Aim, 54
Committee 55-56, 57, 60,

166
Disaster, 54
Group, 55
Plan, 54
Currency Notes, 9
Cyanide, 170

Dallas, 142
Dead Bolt System, 20
Delhi, 68
Detection Equipment,
Electronic Stethoscope, 72
Fibre Scope, 72
Metal Detector, 72
Particle Detection System, 72
Vapour, 72
Wire/Cable Detector, 72
X-Ray, 72
Devil's Advocate, 56
Diplomatic Missions Property, 109, 111
Diplomatic Protection Service, 111
Diplomats, 110-111
Kidnapping, 109
Disturbed Area, 28
Donald, Gloria, 88-90
Door Frame Metal Detector, 33
Doraiswamy, 67
Double Cylinder Locks, 20
Drills,
Evacuation, 33
Fire, 33
Drug Peddling, 68
Drugs, 7
Dundon, 88-90
Electronic Triggering System, 75
Emergencies, 22
First Aid Kid, 23
Emergency,
Drills, 95
Exit, 31
Response Team, 126
Environment, 4
Environmentalist Activists, 3
Escort Car, 83, 105
Executive, 27, 29-31, 35-36, 39, 47, 48, 54, 56, 57, 60-62, 66-67, 76, 81-82, 99, 110, 165, 166
Ex-patriate, 166
Political, 117-118, 120, 126-28, 133, 143
Political Assassination, 117-118
Executive Aircraft, Precaution, 51
Explosive Device, 5
Explosives, 45, 47-48, 51, 71-72, 75-76, 80, 81, 126, 165
Detonator, 72
Gelatine Sticks, 72
Grenades, 72
Improvished Devices, (IED), 72, 73
Mines, 72
Ordnance Devices(EOD), 72
Planting, 45
Plastic, 80
Power Source, 72

Switch, 72
Extortion, 5
Product, 5
Extortionist, 168, 169
Extradiction, 110
Extremes, 66

Fascist, 68
Father of Nation, 153
Fax Machines, 33
FBI Guidelines, 96
Ferdinand Archduke (Austria), 136
Fire Arms, 31, 71, 96, 104
Fire Extinguishers, 23, 25
Fire Stations, 13, 38, 52
Foreign Travel, Precaution, 52-53
Frederick Heineken Case, 91-93
Frisking, 33
Fundamentalists, 117

Gandhi, Indira, 155
Garfield, 132-133
Golden Temple, 158
Gorlogoz, Leon, 134
Government Treasures, 67, 82
Guard Dogs, 18, 19
Guard of Honour, 155
Guatemala, 88
Guilded Hall of Music, 134
Guiteau, Charles, 131, 133

Hague, 92
Handcuffs, 7
Heineken, Freddie, 91
Hideouts, 8
Hijackings, 5, 48-51, 127, 165
Aircraft, 5
Ships, 5
Trains, 5
Hinges, 20
Hit,
List, 105
Team, 7
Hoax Calls, 75
Hobbies, 14
Holy Shrine, 158
Home Security Checklist, 23-26
Hong Kong, 88
Hosni Zaim, 129
Hostage, 8, 15, 10, 61, 63, 64, 69, 109-111, 113, 165
Negotiations, 60, 62, 64, 65
Taking, 4, 5
Human Bomb, 75

Industrial Relations, 62
Industrialist, 3
International Terrorist Group,
Badder-Meinhof, 67
Hezbollah, 67
Irish National Army, 67
LTTE, 67
Palestinian Liberation Organization, 67
Red Army Grade, 67
Intimidation, 5
Iranian MIlitant, 113

Jackson, Andrew, 130
Jackson, Sir Geoffrey, 112, 113

Jammu & Kashmir Liberation Front(JKLF), 66-67
Japan, 166
Japanese Ambassador, 111
Jenkins, Brian, 90
Juan, 84

K.G.B., 73
Karm Chand, 154
Kenneddy, John F., 129, 142, 144
Kevlar Fabrics, 41
Khalistan or Sikh Militant, 66
Khomeini, Ayattollah, 113
Kidnap, 84, 91, 93, 95
Kidnappers, 7-9, 15, 36, 56, 60-61, 63-64, 69, 84-86, 89-90, 93, 110, 112
Kidnapping, 3, 4, 7-11, 15, 17, 27, 35-36, 38, 42, 45, 54, 56, 60-61, 65, 68, 82-83, 91, 93, 94, 104, 109
  Anti-Development, 4
  Seven Phases, 6
    Abduction, 7
    Baruah, 67
    Detention in Hideont, 8
    Doraiswamy, 67
    Negotiations, 9
    Protective, 17
    Ransom Collection, 9
    Reconnaissance and Surveillance, 6, 7, 10
    Release of Hostage, 9
    Rado, 67
    Target Selection, 6
King Abdullah (Jordon), 129
King Fiazal, 129
Kosygin (P.M.)(USSR), 146

LTTE, 155, 160
Labour Policies, 84
Latin America, 82-83, 110
Lawrence, Richard, 130
Leon Don Richard Son - Kidnapping Case, 87-91
Letter Bomb, 80
Letter Bomb Detector, 33, 81
Lift, 30
Lincon, Abraham, 131

Mafia, 5
  Italy, 68
  USA, 68
Mars Chocolate, 170
Mass Media, 110
Mckinley (USA), 134
Media, 79, 168
  Policy, 56
Mega Corporations, 65
Metal Detector, 30, 71
Mercedes, Benz, 104
Miami, 137
Middle East, 110
Military Installation, 13
Miscreants, 3-6, 11-12, 17, 22, 27, 31, 45, 47-50, 55, 65, 66, 69-70, 72, 75, 80,

82, 91, 111, 136, 167, 170
Missiles, 71
Mobile Radio Van, 28
MONTONEROS, 82, 84
Moro, Mr. Aldo, 104-105
Mortars, 71
Moyne, Lord, 138
Mohammed Daoud, 129
Murphy's Law - 15, 124
Mutilation, 8

NSG, 103
Napalm, 74
National Government, 55, 70
National Security, 54
Natural Disasters, 54
Natural Disasters, 54
Natural Disasters, 54
Negotiations Stages, 64
Ethics, 65
Insurance, 65
Policy of Non-Negotiation, 65
Negotiator, 62-65, 83, 89
Neo-Nazi, 68
Niehons, William
Kidnapping Case Study, 85-87
No Asylum Policy, 110
No Negotiation Policy, 110

Organised Crime, 3, 5, 65, 66
Oswald, Lee Harvey, 143

Palestinian, 147
Park Chung Hee, 129
Peace Accord (Sri Lanka), 155
Peepholes, 24
Perimeter Security, 126
Wall, 24
Perpetrators, 167, 170
Personal Attack, 5
Distrcrs Alarm, 31
Documents, 52
Protection -
Assessment of Threats, 11
Planning, 11
Personnel, 99
Security Professionals, 11
Physical Objects,
Buildings, 71
Security Checklist, 32-33
Trains, 71
Poisoning, 126
Police, 28, 37, 52, 60-61, 76, 78, 82, 84-86, 93-94, 104, 111, 127, 165-166, 168-69
Control Room, 30
Dutch, 92
Informer, 156
Officers, 62
Stations, 13, 22, 38, 92
Political
Dignatories, 99
Extremists People War Group (AP), 67
Manifesto, 86
Violent Movement, 82
Popular Caliber, 70
Power Source,

Chemical Timers, 72
Mechanical, 72
Pull, 72
Release, 72
Remote, 72
Timing Devices, 72
Time Pencil, 72
Pranksters, 75
Prevention Equipment,
Bomb Blanket, 73
Bomb Suits, 73
Electronic Frequency
Jammers, 73
Preventive Measures,
Chauffer, 39
Road Journey, 35-39
Route Variation, 38
Vulnerable Areas, 38
Prime Minister of Jordon, 14
Princip, Gavrilo, 136
Principles of Protection, 120-121
Access Control, 120
Concentric Circles, 120
Protection,
Children, 96-97
Executives, 99
Family, 95
Money, 5
Personal, 99, 133
Rackets, 5
Women, 98
Protective Arrangements,
Blue Prints, 123, 124
Communication, 22
Curtain, 21
Direct Defensive
Measures, 122
Domestic Servant, 22
Fire Arms, 22
Guidelines Location, 17
Hinges, 20
Indirect Defensive
Measures, 122
Integrated Chain, 123
Lighting, 21
Locks, 20
Perimeter Security, 18
Planning, 123
Security Guards, 19
Professional Conduct and
Operating Procedures, 101
Prostitution, 68
Psycho-Analysis, 64
Psychologists, 87
Public Relation Staff, 12
Publicity, 165, 166
Pump Action Shot-Guns, 22

Radicals, 3, 4
Radio Active Elements, 74
Rabin, Yitzhak, 156
Rado, 67
Rajghat, 153
Ransome, 3,9,10, 17, 60, 61, 64-65, 67-68, 83-84, 91, 93, 95, 114, 167, 169
Rawalpindi, 141
Reagon, R, 99
Red Cross, 93
Rehman, Mujibur, 129
Remote Control, 45
Resistence, 96
Risk Quotient, 123
Rockets, 71
Rohana, WV, 155

Roosevelt, F.D., 137
Roosevelt, Theodore, 135

Sabotage, 5, 21, 127, 166
Safe Havens, 23, 25, 95
Safe Travel Guidelines, 43-44
Sarajevo, 136
Schleyer, Hans Martin, 104
Schrank, John, 135
Science and Technology, 70
Secret Service Agent, 134, 143
Secretaries, 12, 23
Secretary, 30, 51, 61, 76, 81
Security,
  Aircraft, 127
  Airport, 48
  Alarms, 30
  Baggage, 127
  Food and Drinks, 127
  Offices 29-31
  Runway, 127
  Service Crew, 127
Self-Defence Squads, 166
Sikh Militancy, 158
Sikh Security Personnel, 159
Silencers, 71
Sinclair, Kevin, 90
Sirens, 39
Smadhi, Mahatma Gandhi, 153
Social Functions, 7
Society Chronicles, 6
Somarama, 142
Sources of Threat, 3
Sniffer Dogs, 78
Special Counter Terrorist Force, 55
Special Interest Group Terrorist,
  Animal Welfare Group, 67, 165-166
  Anti-Abortion 67, 165-166
  Anti-Nuclear Group, 67, 165-166
  Environmental, 67, 165, 166
SPG, 103
Stockholm Syndrome, 8
Subsidiary Factors,
  Family History, 6
  Wealthy Connection, 6
Sunsilk Shampoo, 169
Surveillance, 13, 36-37, 62, 101-102, 110, 123
  Fixed, 12, 13
  Foot, 12
  Vehicle, 12, 13
Swiss Bank Account, 9
Switzerland, 84
Sydney Stores, 168
Syed Akbhar, 141

Telephones, 60-61
Telescopes, 71
Terrorists, 3, 65, 66, 85, 86, 105, 110, 113-114, 158, 160, 165, 167
  International Groups, 66, 70
  National Groups, 66, 70
  Soft-Terrorist, 165
Texas School Book Depository, 143

Threats, 39, 63, 74, 75, 76, 78, 79, 95, 117-18, 123, 126, 156
Bomb, 5, 29, 33, 166, 167
Contaminated Goods, 165
Explosives, 29
Level, 45
Meetings, 35
Reporting Room, 79
Special Groups, 165-166
Tolbert, William, 130
Torresolo and Collazo, 140
Toxic Chemical Agents(Man Made), 73
Training of Children, 96
Trauma Kit, 99
Trujillo, Rafael, 129
Truman, Harry, S, 140
Tsafendes, 144
Tylenol (USA), 170

U Saw, 139
Underground Tunnels, 8
United Kingdom, 166
United Liberation Front Assam, (ULFA), 67

Vandalism, 5
Vehicle Selection, 40-41
Venezuela, 85-86
Verwoerd, Henrick, 144
VIP Complex, 118

Warning,
Buttons, 30
Panic, 31
System, Anti Tamper, 39, 45
Warren Commission, 143
Weapons,
Automatic, 71, 88, 139
Pistol, 71
Revolvers, 71
Western Europe, 166
White Phosphorons, 74
White Slave Traffic, 68
World War I, 136

Zangara, Guisseppe, 137
Zero Defect Situation, 125
Zia-ur-Rahman, 130